LIFE AFTER GRACE

D0833155

Glimpses of Glory: Daily Reflections on the Bible
Carol M. Bechtel

"Sometimes all it takes is a glimpse to keep us going. A navigator catches sight of the north star and corrects the ship's course. We look in the eyes of someone who understands us, and we can face what is ahead with renewed courage. *Glimpses of Glory* seeks to give us such glimpses into the Bible. Sometimes what we see will startle; sometimes it will console. Sometimes it will delight us with its humanity; other times it will drive us to our knees with its divinity. But always the glimpse will invite us into a more intimate relationship with the Bible and the God who is revealed to us in it."

—from the Preface

This rich collection of stories provides fertile ground for anyone who wants to be on more intimate terms with the Bible. Inspiring and uplifting, these meditations are ideal for those seeking to grow in personal faith and Bible knowledge. Each meditation is followed by questions for discussion and reflection, which make this a book that is easily adaptable for both individual or group use.

Westminster John Knox Press
$12.95
0-664-25743-7

Call 1-800-227-2872 to order.

LIFE AFTER GRACE

Daily Reflections on the Bible

Carol M. Bechtel

Westminster John Knox Press
LOUISVILLE • LONDON

Scripture quotations, unless otherwise indicated, are from the New Revised Standard Version of the Bible, copyright © 1989 by the Division of Christian Education of the National Council of the Churches of Christ in the U.S.A., and used by permission.

Portions of the Bible study on Job 42, "The Courage to Be," are from a series of Bible studies on the book of Job by Carol Bechtel, published by the Adult Foundational Curriculum in 1997.

Book design by Sharon Adams
Cover design by Night & Day Design

First edition
Published by Westminster John Knox Press
Louisville, Kentucky

This book is printed on acid-free paper that meets the American National Standards Institute Z39.48 standard. ♾

PRINTED IN THE UNITED STATES OF AMERICA

03 04 05 06 07 08 09 10 11 12 — 10 9 8 7 6 5 4 3 2 1

Library of Congress Cataloging-in-Publication Data

Bechtel, Carol M., 1959–
    Life after grace : daily reflections on the Bible / Carol M. Bechtel.
      p. cm.
  Includes index.
  ISBN 0-664-22311-7 (alk. paper)
  1. Bible—Meditations.   2. Spiritual life—Christianity—Meditations.
  3. Devotional calendars.   I. Title.

BS491.3.B43   2003
242'.5—dc21   2002192255

To Tom Mullens,
my partner in life and grace

Contents

Preface

*S*ixteenth-century saint Theresa of Avila once took God to task for allowing her to suffer so much. God is said to have replied, "But Theresa, that is how I treat all my friends." Without missing a beat, Theresa shot back, "Then Lord, it is no wonder you have so few."

Theresa's story, whether apocryphal or not, points out that the Christian life is not without its perils. Rather than deflecting the slings and arrows of outrageous fortune, sometimes becoming a Christian seems to launch them in our direction. Yet, we can hardly accuse Jesus of false advertising. "Take up your cross and follow me" is not exactly an invitation to a luxury cruise.

So, why does anyone sign on for this particular path of faith? And what can we expect when we do?

The answer to the first question is best boiled down to one word: grace. We come to Christ because he offers us "grace that is greater than all our sin." That one extravagant offer pulls the rug out from under all our efforts to work our way into God's good graces. Whether we make it to the baptismal font under our own steam or in the arms of our parents, the grace that reaches out to embrace us is the same. But what can Christians expect after that?

Many Christians don't seem particularly worried about what life after grace is like. Their concern for being "saved" seems to eclipse all that comes after. Other Christians offer false promises of success and security, as if our faith somehow obligates God to reward us in the world's terms. This book seeks to address both misunderstandings. Its emphasis on what happens *after* God's initial act of grace highlights that being a Christian is more than having one's card punched. Its honest assessment of the challenges that believers face argues against the idea that faith can be used as a means to a material end.

Life after Grace, then, traces the tests, tribulations, and victories of believers in both the Old and New Testaments *after* their experience of God's saving grace. In theological terms, the book is a short course in sanctification (as opposed to justification). But in simple terms, this small volume presents a series of biblical snapshots on themes that confront every Christian somewhere along the way . . . themes like forgiveness, self-deception, care of creation, suffering, call, discord, and hope. Each snapshot seeks to offer some insight into both the believer and the Bible, pointing to ways we can all grow in grace. Each snapshot illustrates the very real ways that life *after* grace is really life *within* grace. As the last study in the book points out, God's goodness and mercy pursue us *all* the days of our lives.

This book has much in common with its predecessor, *Glimpses of Glory* (Westminster John Knox Press, 1998). Both books are based on Bible studies that were originally written for *Presbyterians Today.* Both follow a similar format. Each meditation is based on a short Scripture passage that should be read along with the study. (The New Revised Standard Version is a helpful and reliable translation and is used for all quotes in the studies unless otherwise indicated.) Questions for discussion or reflection follow, making this book easily adaptable for either individual or group use.

Many readers of *Glimpses of Glory* indicated that they were, in fact, using the book for weekly or monthly Bible study groups. With this information in mind, I have included hymn suggestions for each study in *Life after Grace*. Even if your group is not musically inclined, remember that many hymns make excellent prayers. A verse or two could well provide an opening or closing prayer. I have chosen hymns from a range of denominational collections in the hope that groups can access at least one with ease.

The inclusion of hymn suggestions should also make the book a ready resource for preachers and worship planners. To this end, I have also included an index of all the primary Scripture passages referenced in the studies.

The book is divided into three sections of ten studies each. The first section, "Life after Grace," lends its title and its theme to the book as a whole. The section's focus is on what Christians can expect after the first blush of belief has worn off. Contrary to the mistaken assumption that once we are "saved" we can sit back and relax, these studies explore both the work and the wonder that awaits us on the other side of baptism.

The second set of studies focuses on "Close Encounters" between believers and the God they are coming to know. Not surprisingly, these studies often urge us toward greater self-knowledge as well.

The third section, "Practicing the Faith," explores some of the issues that exercise us spiritually as we seek to grow in Christ. Characters from Genesis to Revelation illustrate that, while it is hard work, practicing has profound spiritual rewards.

Speaking of hard work, Catherine Cottingham deserves recognition here for all of hers during the years I wrote for *Presbyterians Today*. Her patience, encouragement, and editing made every study in this book better. Finally, I would like to thank all of the teachers, students, colleagues, friends, and family who have helped me grow in grace over the years. You know who you are. God bless you.

Carol Bechtel
All Saints' Day 2002

List of Hymnals
and Abbreviations

SNC   *Sing! A New Creation*
         New York, New York: Reformed Church Press
         Grand Rapids, Michigan: Calvin Institute of
             Christian Worship
         Grand Rapids, Michigan: CRC Publications, 2001

UMH   *The United Methodist Hymnal*
         Nashville, Tennessee: The United Methodist
             Publishing House, 1989

Life After Grace

The Faith to Go Forward

Exodus 14:10–31

*P*retend just for a moment that you do not know how the story of the Exodus turns out. Pretend that you do not know that God's people do indeed "pass with unmoisted foot through the Red Sea waters."

Now, picture yourself on the banks of that sea. Under other circumstances you might enjoy the scenery, but you're not on a nature hike. The fact of the matter is, you and all the people you love are lined up as for a firing squad. At your backs is an impassible body of water. The dust from the desert and the rumbling of the chariot wheels announce the impending arrival of your executioners. You have no escape. Today is the last day in the life of the newly liberated people of God.

The irony is not lost on some of your traveling companions. "Is it because there were no graves in Egypt that you have taken us away to die in the wilderness?" they ask Moses with grim sarcasm.

Charlton Heston's Moses may have approached this predicament with unshakable confidence, but the Bible's Moses looks a little less self-assured. At the very end of an otherwise stirring speech, he tells his frightened followers, "The LORD will fight for you, and you have only to keep still."

God, in fact, has a more active agenda in mind for the Israelites. "Why do you cry out to me?" he asks Moses. "Tell the Israelites to go forward."

If this scene were from an old Bill Cosby skit, Moses would raise incredulous eyes toward heaven and, after an awkward pause, ask, "Say what?"

The suggestion is absurd. Go forward *where?* "Lift up your staff, and stretch out your hand over the sea and divide it," God tells Moses matter-of-factly, "that the Israelites may go into the sea on dry ground."

This situation is one of those good news/bad news times in Scripture that we can only really appreciate if we enter into the story as participants. Imagine the thrill of wonder as you feel God's breath on your face and see the waters begin to part. Yet, imagine the thrill of fear when you realize that God means for you to walk between those walls of water.

What are your options here, really? You can't very well go back, since Pharaoh is practically breathing down your neck already. This fact pretty much eliminates the possibility of standing still, as well, though we should probably allow for at least a few minutes of the "deer in the headlights" effect. That leaves stepping out into that sandy path through the sea. The option is not an attractive one, but it may well be the least *unattractive* of the three.

I once heard veteran New Haven preacher Doug Nelson preach on this passage. Though good ten years have passed since I heard the sermon, I'll never forget what he said. The real miracle of the Red Sea, Doug suggested, was not that the waters parted, but *that the people went forward*.

Doug was also the person who said, "When you pray, you'd better get ready to duck."

Prayer is funny like that, as Moses and the Israelites discovered that day on the banks of the sea. When we cry out to God, God sometimes answers in ways that are absolutely terrifying. As Barbara Brown Taylor reminds us, the Bible "is a book in which wonderful and terrible things happen by the power of an *almighty* God, whose steadfast love for us does not seem to preclude scaring the living daylights out of us from time to time." (*The Preaching Life*, Cowley Publications, 59)

Yet, finally, we do not step out into the sea alone. God is with us, which makes all the difference. And God, finally, is the one who gives us the courage for that first step of faith.

Think of this passage the next time you find yourself in a situation where you can't go back, you can't stand still, and you're terrified to go forward. Then say your prayers and step forward in faith, trusting that you will indeed experience life after grace.

For Reflection

1. Have you ever been in a situation like this? What did you do? Do you wish you'd responded differently?
2. When you pray, do you get ready to duck? Why or why not?
3. What would you tell a new Christian about God's penchant for "scaring the living daylights out of us from time to time"?

Hymn Suggestions

"Come Ye Faithful, Raise the Strain" (CH 215; GC 441; H 199, 200; HPSS 114, 115; LBW 132; NCH 230; PsH 389; RIL 315, 316; UMH 315)

"Here I Am, Lord" (GC 686; HPSS 525; SNC 268; UMH 593)

Law As Grace

Exodus 20:1–17

*A*nn Landers once reprinted a list of several rules for raising a juvenile delinquent. High on the list was: "Begin in infancy to give the child everything he [or she] wants."

This ironic advice has a lot of practical wisdom behind it. Children need limits that are gently, firmly, and fairly enforced if they are to grow up with any sense of security or boundaries. Little Tiffany will never make the Olympic team, for instance, if she is allowed to sit on the couch and eat candy all day. Little Tommy might learn a painful lesson if he pulls the cat's tail once too often. Busy streets, swimming pools, and smiling strangers are all things that must be negotiated with a certain amount of caution.

We don't stop needing limits when we grow up. Too much of a good thing can kill us every bit as quickly as a small dose of the demonic.

Perhaps God's own awareness of this concept led to the giving of the Ten Commandments (see Exod. 20:1–17; also Deut. 5:6–21). As Tom Troeger's beautiful hymn reminds us,

> The line, the limit, and the law
>> Are patterns meant to help us draw
> A bound between what life requires
>> And all the things our heart desires.
> We are not free when we're confined
>> To every wish that sweeps the mind,
> But free when freely we accept

>The sacred bounds that must be kept.
>(from "God Marked a Line
>and Told the Sea," 1986)

In a very real sense, then, the Ten Commandments are a gift from God, given with our own best interests at heart. To flaunt these loving limits is to invite incalculable anguish into our lives and the lives of those around us. In this sense, law *is* grace.

Yet, these ancient injunctions offer another gracious dimension. We may not be able to see it, however, unless we look at the larger story of which they are a part.

Take a moment and imagine yourself as an ancient Israelite. You have just been introduced to the Lord of the Universe. Some people are saying that this God is the same one who led your ancestors around, but that may be nothing more than a rumor. For some inscrutable reason, this cosmic God has taken an interest in your people and liberated you from slavery in Egypt.

Ancient Israelite etiquette clearly holds that you really need to send some sort of thank-you offering to this God. Besides, you really are grateful. But you remember what happened to those poor Egyptians who tried to chase you through the Red Sea. Being on the wrong side of this deity could be dangerous; one wouldn't want to send the wrong thing. Suppose you send pork chops and God prefers chicken salad? What's a grateful Israelite to do?

What is a grateful believer of each era to do? Like the ancient Israelites, we have been the recipients of God's liberating love. We have passed through the waters of baptism and have been raised to "walk in the newness of life" (Rom. 6:4). How can we show our gratitude to God for "this grace in which we stand" (Rom. 5:2)?

In the Ten Commandments, God shows us how to say "thank you." No more eloquent and appropriate thanksgiving exists, after all, than a life lived in grateful obedience to God.

This way of viewing the commandments offers a crucial complement to the usual depiction of the law as a means of convicting us of our sin. While the law does indeed function in this more negative sense, the Bible provides a basis for seeing the law as the "carrot" as well as the "stick." For those people who know that they are justified "not by the works of the law but through faith in Jesus Christ" (Gal. 2:15), obedience becomes a blessing rather than a burden. The commandments become a crucial guide for life after grace.

For Reflection

1. Do you tend to think of the Ten Commandments as a blessing or a burden?
2. Is your obedience grounded in gratitude or fear? Does it matter? How?
3. How do the values expressed in Tom Troeger's hymn compare to cultural values that emphasize self-fulfillment? What does fulfillment mean for a Christian?

Hymn Suggestions

"God Marked a Line and Told the Sea" (HPSS 283; NCH 568)

"The Lord Is God, There Is No Other" (RIL 65; cf. PsH 153)

"Come, Thou Font of Every Blessing" (CH 16; H 686; HPSS 356; LBW 499; PsH 486; UMH 400; RIL 449)

"Let All Things Now Living" (GC 567; HPSS 554; LBW 557; PsH 453)

"Psalm 19; God's Glory Fills the Heavens" (SNC 88; cf. PsH 19 and GC 489)

Guilt, Grace, and Golden Calves

Exodus 32

*S*o few of us feel the urge to worship golden calves these days—unless, of course, they are the kind one can acquire with the aid of a running track and a tanning booth.

Yet, once we move beyond the literalism of actual calf worship, we realize that the urge to "lift up our souls to that which is false" is a fairly timeless tendency. And if we are to believe Exodus 32, the tendency can surface even in the believing community's worship services.

Finding fault with these ungrateful Israelites is easy. Though they can still taste the salt of the Red Sea on their lips, they are quick to forget the one who rescued them from their Egyptian overlords. When Aaron obligingly unveils the golden calf that the people have begged for in Moses' absence, the people shout, "These are your gods, O Israel, who brought you up out of the land of Egypt!"

The effrontery of this theological sleight of hand is mind-boggling. "What are they thinking?" we ask as we read, shaking our heads sanctimoniously.

Before we become too smug, however, we ought to notice that what they are thinking about is not entirely clear. Aaron, at least, seems to have some notion that the people can still worship the one true God in the guise of this calf. "Tomorrow shall be a festival *to the LORD*," he proclaims in verse 5 (italics added). Maybe he is just trying to make the best out of a bad situation. But whatever his reasons, the Bible leaves just a hint of ambiguity in the story at this point. We as readers can never be quite sure who or what the people think they are worshiping.

No matter what their motives, God's reaction is unambiguous. "*Your* people," he announces to Moses (italics added), "whom *you* brought up out of the land of Egypt, have acted perversely" (note the accusatory distancing!). As evidence, God actually quotes the people's cry of acclamation from the unveiling ceremony ("These are your gods, O Israel . . ."). Finally, in a conflagration of rage, God threatens to incinerate the people and start over again with Moses.

By means of three persuasive arguments (All that work for nothing? What would the neighbors say? and You promised . . .), Moses actually succeeds in changing God's mind. Yet, even with this worst-case scenario avoided, a price must still be paid. The rest of the story, as they say, is not pretty. In the unforgettably graphic words of seventeenth-century preacher Joseph Hall, Moses

> burns and stamps the calf to powder, and gives it [to] Israel to drink, that they might have it in their belly, instead of their eyes . . . that, instead of going before Israel it might pass through them, so the next day they might find their god in their excrements. (*Contemplations of the Historical Passages*, Book V)

When Moses confronts Aaron with his lack of leadership, Aaron tries to downplay his role in the debacle by trying to make it sound as if the calf jumped out of the kiln of its own accord. The Levites then earn their ordination as a priestly tribe by slaughtering—at Moses' command—every "brother, friend, and neighbor" who refuses to repent. Finally, a plague from God sweeps through the camp. Not even the repentant, evidently, escape completely unscathed.

This picture of life after grace is pretty grim, but its realism is instructive. The people of God are not immune to temptation. In fact, if we take this story seriously, we realize that temptation sometimes strikes while the taste of the communion wine is still on our lips. Popular culture's values and assumptions creep into our very worship. Congregations become audiences, sin is dismissed as a "downer," and we much prefer a God built to our own specifications. Hymnwriter Henry Twells has a word for all of us gathered worshipfully around such golden calves. He writes:

> Not for our sins alone thy mercy, Lord, we sue;
> let fall thy pitying glance on our devotions too,
> what we have done for thee, and what we think to do.
> The holiest hours we spend in prayer upon our knees,
> the times when most we deem our songs of praise will
>   please,
> thou searcher of all hearts, forgiveness pour on these.

For Reflection

1. How do the values of popular culture shape worship services in your congregation? Is such influence always a bad thing? Why or why not? How do we tell?
2. When are you most vulnerable to temptation? Why?
3. Why do you think the people of God were so quick to give their new god the credit for the exodus?

Hymn Suggestions

"As a Chalice Cast of Gold" (CH 287; HPSS 336)
"Not for Our Sins Alone" (RIL 506)
"I Greet Thee, Who My Sure Redeemer Art" (HPSS 457; NCH 251; PsH 248; RIL 366)
"Gather Us In" (GC 744; SNC 8)
"For the Bread Which You Have Broken" (CH 411; H 342; HPSS 508, 509; LBW 200; RIL 547; UMH 614, 615)

I Once Was Blind

Mark 10:46–52

I had been sitting on that roadside for years, begging and blind. The road was good for begging, as far as that goes, with a fair amount of traffic, especially around holy days. I could always count on those pious religious pilgrims to lighten their conscience along with their purse. That may sound calculating, but let's face it: it's a harsh world out there, especially if you're Bartimaeus, the blind beggar.

The world was never so harsh as on the day I was healed.

A large crowd was approaching, which was usually a good sign from my perspective. But my initial hopes were checked by the sound of the voices. This crowd was not just any crowd. They had an agenda. The tension was high, although the reason wasn't clear. They sounded as if they couldn't decide whether they were on their way to an execution or a party.

Then someone near me shouted, "There he is . . . the rabbi from Nazareth!" Suddenly I understood. I had heard about Jesus. According to some, he was a dangerous man to be with; but to listen to others, he was a dangerous man to be without. I hadn't quite made up my mind yet. Or at least, I wasn't aware that I had.

But then, I heard the sound of my own voice rising above the shouts of the people around me. I don't know what got into me, but suddenly, what had started out as a prayer under my breath was a full-fledged shout. "Jesus, Son of David, have mercy on me!"

I'm not sure who was more anxious to shut me up. Some of the voices were familiar. My friends (such as I had) were embarrassed, I suppose, at my making such a fuss, but I think some of the people trying to shush me may have been his disciples. Maybe they thought my use of that messianic title, Son of David, would light the fuse under the procession's powder keg. They could well have been right, because some of the other voices began to turn really ugly at that point.

But then another voice carried across the crowd. Perhaps the reason I heard it was that its tone was so different, or maybe it was because it was *his* voice. I guess I'll never know. In any case, clearly I was not calling him anymore. He was calling me.

It's funny how accommodating everyone became all of a sudden. The very people who had tried to silence me just moments before were now shoving me forward. What were they thinking, I wonder? The religious authorities may have been trying to set a trap for him. His disciples were probably looking for a diversion. In either case, it didn't matter. I followed the sound of his voice.

I was so intent on his voice, as a matter of fact, that I did something completely out of character: I threw off my cloak and hurried toward him. Normally, I would never have left my cloak, especially in a crowd like this. What were the chances that I would be able to find it again? And I can't remember the last time I hurried like that, heedless of every obstacle.

The sudden stillness told me that I had found him. But then I might as well have been struck dumb as well as blind. I couldn't find any words to say.

He was the one who finally broke the silence. "What do you want me to do for you?" he asked. The question was so direct, it was disarming.

What *did* I want? For years I had prayed for the strength to endure my suffering . . . the grace to bear my blindness with a better attitude. But now . . . I guess I never expected God to show up in the flesh and ask me that question point-blank.

In a heartbeat I knew what I wanted. I wanted to be healed—really healed. And I knew that if I didn't ask him now, I might never have another chance. I screwed up my courage and said, "My teacher, let me see again."

Making that request was my last act as a blind beggar.

My faith has made me well, he says. If that's true, then my sight bears witness to the fact that faith is a gift. But however the healing happened, I know that life after grace is going to be radically different. I have no choice now but to follow . . . even if the road leads to Jerusalem . . . even if the road leads to a cross. I once was blind, but now I see.

For Reflection

1. What do you want God to do for you? What if God says no? What if God says yes?
2. How do we know whether to pray for patience or healing? Can we be too timid in our prayers? too bold?
3. How do you respond when someone suggests that a lack of healing reflects a lack of faith?

Hymn Suggestions

"Just as I Am, without One Plea" (CH 339; H 693; HPSS 370; LBW 296; NCH 207; PsH 263; RIL 467, 468; UMH 357)
"O Christ, the Healer" (CH 503; HPSS 380; LBW 360; NCH 175; UMH 265)
"Jesus, Heal Us" (GC 875)
"Psalm 40; Wait for the Lord" (GC 332; SNC 96)

Blessed Mourners

Matthew 5:4

*N*ew Christians tend to become nervous around passages like Matthew 5:4. They've just wheeled their new faith into the driveway. Before they can even pull the sticker off the window, this passage implies dings and dents and damage control. Matthew 5:4 is a shock, but perhaps we are better off bearing it sooner rather than later in our journey through life after grace. Faith apparently does not necessarily protect us from pain, disgrace, or disaster. Passages like these help us to prepare for the inevitable.

"Blessed are those who mourn," says Jesus blithely from the mountainside.

"What did he say?" The whispered questions must have run like ripples through the gathered crowd. "He couldn't have said that, could he? What planet is this man from? Surely, we must have misheard. . . ."

The ripples still run through the ranks of gathered Christians today. We still struggle to understand what Jesus could have meant by calling mourners "blessed." Indeed, some translations make the statement even more shocking by rendering the word "happy." Happy mourners? Try telling that to the young couple whose two-year-old son has just drowned in a hot tub. Try telling that to the family whose sixteen-year-old daughter came home from a fishing trip in a coma.

Some people have suggested that this and the other so-called "beatitudes" point primarily toward the future.

According to this way of reading, their meaning and their comfort lie in the way they reassure us that God is working to bring us to that day when mourners *will* be comforted. Surely, the future tense is important here, in that it does point to a time when God will wipe every tear from our eyes (Rev. 7:17; 21:4) and turn our mourning into dancing (Ps. 30:11). Nick Wolterstorff describes this kind of forward focus in his painfully personal book, *Lament for a Son* (Eerdmans, 1987, 85). Wolterstorff sees the mourners as "those who have caught a glimpse of God's new day, who ache with all their being for that day's coming, and who break out into tears when confronted with its absence."

Still, the present tense is important as well, and deserves better than a back seat in our struggle to interpret Jesus' words. "Blessed are those who mourn," it says, after all. But where, pray tell, could that blessing be?

Perhaps one blessed oasis in the miserable experience of mourning is in giving us the opportunity to experience God's comfort. While this concept in no way serves as an explanation for suffering, this observation is made somewhat timidly by many an exhausted mourner. We would never have wished for this experience, and we would most certainly never wish it on anyone else. But there is a certain exquisite sadness in knowing the weeping embrace of a God who suffers with us.

Close to this experience is the realization that grief and mourning often produce more profound Christians. While not always the case (some become lost in bitterness and despair), the result happens often enough to take note of it.

My friend Eleanor watched her husband's plane crash and burn. She was a wonderful person before that horrible loss. But now, ten years later, she is a profound person as well. Suffering has refined her faith, searing out the easy answers and the pious platitudes. She is one of the first people I turn to when I have something or someone to mourn.

John Bell of Scotland's Iona Community once observed that no one becomes a deeply spiritual person by receiving everything they want. Spirituality, Bell points out, "is not produced in a life which is pleasure-filled and pain free." Indeed, in the mysterious economy of God, "the bane is part of the blessing" (from a lecture at Western Theological Seminary, Holland, Michigan, July 25, 1997).

Perhaps this real and present blessing is what the hymn writer, William Cowper, had in mind when he wrote: "Ye fearful saints, fresh courage take—the clouds ye so much dread are big with mercy, and shall break with blessings on your head" ("God Moves in a Mysterious Way," 1774). In any case, I am wondering whether we ought to replace our opening analogy of Christian faith as a "new car" with one comparing Christians to fine furniture. Furniture, after all, only becomes more valuable with age and "antiquing."

For Reflection

1. In your own experience, has mourning ever been "blessed"? Why and how?
2. What are the risks of reminding others that they are "blessed" in their time of mourning?
3. Why are new Christians so often surprised by the harsh realities of the Christian life? What can mature Christians do to help them?

Hymn Suggestions

"What Wondrous Love Is This" (CH 200; GC 627; HPSS 85; LBW 385; NCH 223; PsH 379; SNC 142; UMH 292)

"Near to the Heart of God" (CH 581; HPSS 527: UMH 472)

"God Moves in a Mysterious Way" (H 677; HPSS 270; LBW 483; NCH 412; PsH 434; RIL 36)

Stop, Look, and Listen

Numbers 22:1–40

*T*alking animals are big these days. What with computer technology and sophisticated new strides in animation, we hardly even bat an eye when Babe the talking pig carries on a conversation with a herd of recalcitrant sheep. At least back in the 1960s we had the grace to act surprised when Mr. Ed, the talking horse, flapped his lips and said, "Wilburrrr."

So why isn't Balaam surprised when his donkey suddenly sits down in the middle of the road and gives him a piece of her mind?

Maybe it's because the donkey is talking sense.

Balaam is a man on a mission, though he is none too happy about it. The king of Moab has summoned him to come and put a curse on the Israelites, who have camped a little too close for Moabite comfort. Even though Balaam is not an Israelite himself, he seems to have a healthy respect for the Israelite God. So, in spite of the Moabite king's repeated attempts to flatter and bribe, Balaam refuses to curse what God has blessed. He only agrees to accompany the king's messengers after receiving grudging permission from God, who tells him in v. 20, "If the men have come to summon you, get up and go with them; but do only what I tell you to do." Only then does he saddle his infamous ass and set out.

We are brought up short when verse 22 announces that "God's anger was kindled because he was going." Wait a minute. Didn't God just give Balaam permission to do just that?

The Bible is tantalizingly silent about God's sudden change of heart. Yet given the way the story progresses, one wonders if God didn't want to give Balaam an unforgettable object lesson. He is about to receive a vivid reminder that God can speak even through the most unlikely of lips.

As Balaam and his servants make their way toward Moab, they encounter a heavenly roadblock: an angel brandishing a sword. The irony is that the donkey is the only one who sees it. She wisely turns aside into a field. Balaam is not amused, and he strikes her. His anger simmers still hotter when she takes evasive action a second and third time, first scraping his foot against a wall in an attempt to squeeze by the angel and then simply lying down in the middle of the road. When he beats her the third time, she lets him have it, naming him as the ungrateful wretch that he is.

Only then does God open Balaam "the seer's" eyes.

This story packs a couple of surprises for believers who think they have all the answers. Who would have expected a foreign diviner like Balaam to have a genuine word from the Lord, after all? How much less, then, do we expect his ornery donkey to have one! Yet, this ancient story teaches us an important lesson on our journey through life after grace: God's wisdom sometimes comes from unexpected sources.

The Bible is full of such stories—so full, in fact, that they should stop surprising us. Balaam and his talking donkey join the ranks of many "faithful foreigners" who have something to say to the believing community. Rahab, Uriah, and Ruth come to mind from the Old Testament; the centurion of Matthew 8 and the wise men from the east come to mind from the New Testament.

Hearing God speaking to us in an unfamiliar voice is not always easy. When environmentalists squeeze our foot against the wall over the Styrofoam cups we use at the church coffee hour, we see no connection to the hymn we're humming under our breath: "How shall we love thee, holy, hidden

Being, if we love not the world which thou hast made?" (from "Father Eternal, Ruler of Creation," words by Laurence Houseman, 1919).

Balaam's story reminds us to stop, look, and listen for God in the unfamiliar. Perhaps it would help to remember that Jesus himself came as a stranger. The only question is: Will we welcome him?

For Reflection

1. Has God ever spoken to you through an unlikely source? How did it change the way you thought or behaved?
2. How do we—as individuals and as the church—recognize God's voice?
3. Why do you suppose God seems to like speaking through outsiders?

Hymn Suggestions

"Father Eternal, Ruler of Creation" (H 573; LBW 413; RIL 489)

"Open My Eyes That I May See" (CH 586; HPSS 324; UMH 454; cf. SNC 263)

"A Touching Place" (GC 640)

"We Limit Not the Truth of God" (H 629; NCH 316)

"Holy Spirit, Mighty God" (PsH 278)

Deliver Us from Evil

Psalm 36

*T*he sound of their singing was gossamer thin. "No aspiring opera stars here," I thought to myself as I scaled back my own voice to match those of the women around me.

I was the guest of several Episcopal nuns at a small convent in New York City. As darkness descended on the city around us, the sisters had ascended the stairs to their chapel for evening prayer. Candles were lit; psalms were sung. But it wasn't until the closing hymn that I discovered what was really happening.

Comfort every sufferer, watching late in pain, the sisters sang to the tune of "Now the Day Is Over." *Those who plan some evil, from their sin restrain.*

Somewhere in the gathering darkness, plans were being made for evil and not for good. Perhaps the plans would go forward; perhaps they wouldn't. Would the sisters' prayers make the difference? The prospect was startling. For an instant I saw the city suspended on that gossamer thread, the only thing keeping us from falling into the abyss.

The author of Psalm 36 (traditionally David) is suspended by a thread that is equally flimsy. Though thinking of his voice blending with those of some twentieth-century nuns is an odd concept, that is exactly what happens in this psalm. Read it and meet a man who would be very much at home in a candlelit convent in the midst of a dark and dangerous city. Read it and meet a man who would feel very much at home

21

in a world where just sending your children out the door in the morning is an act of faith.

We have a feel in the opening verses of the psalm for what David—and we—are facing. Verses 1–4 read like a poetic police report. They introduce us to public enemy number one: the wicked. These people are as smooth as silk and as sincere as polyester. These people are so self-deceived that they have lost all sense of sin, and thus all capacity for confession. These people lie awake at night rationalizing the most reprehensible behavior. These people can no longer distinguish between right and wrong—or worse, they know the difference but don't care.

Being this candid about the enemy takes courage. The police report is unnerving. Yet, if we expect the psalmist to cower and cry "uncle," we are in for a surprise. Verses 5–6 put things in perspective. As terrifying as the threat is, it is no match for God. The steadfast love of the Lord towers over even the most formidable of enemies. God's justice undergirds the universe, ultimately reassuring us that the wicked will not get away with anything.

Now that we have caught sight of safety, running for cover makes sense. Verses 7–9 picture the faithful scurrying like chicks for the shadow of God's wings. Yet, safety is not the only thing we will find there. God, as it turns out, wants more for us than "just" the absence of evil. Safety is only the start of what we enjoy in God's presence. In fact, we are invited to drink from the river of God's delights. Given that the word for "delights" is related to the noun "Eden," we can assume that God has more in mind for us than bread and water.

Once we have found our way to such a refuge, who could blame us for wanting to stay? And yet, the psalmist seems to know that he—and we—will have to venture forth and become vulnerable once again. Like those Episcopal sisters, we are going to have to go back into an often hostile world on a daily basis—to work, to witness, to live lives of faith-

fulness. Most frightening of all is the realization that sometimes the threat may come from within. At times, God's light
will have to drive away the darkness that has seeped into our
own soul.

In the face of such real and present dangers, the psalmist
concludes with a prayer: deliver us from evil. This defense
may sound flimsy, but by now we ought to realize that the
strength of our prayers will not save us. Rather, the grace of
God saves . . . the grace of a God whose steadfast love is more
than able to keep us from falling.

For Reflection

1. What has this psalm taught you about the life of faith?
2. Have you ever known anyone whose prayers may have
   kept you from falling?
3. How important is praying? How can we know if it does
   any good?

Hymn Suggestions

"Now the Day Is Over" (H 42; HPSS 541; LBW 280;
   NCH 98)
"A Mighty Fortress Is Our God" (CH 65; H 687, 688;
   HPSS 259, 260; NCH 439, 440; PsH 469; RIL 179;
   UMH 110)
"If You Believe and I Believe" (GC 722; cf. SNC 274)

Once More with Feeling

2 Samuel 12:1–14

*D*avid's indignation was genuine. The prophet Nathan had just related a story that had offended all of his finer instincts. A rich man, it seems, had served up a poor man's pet lamb for lunch. "As the LORD lives," swears David with all the power vested in his royal office, "the man who has done this deserves to die" (v. 5). David slumps back on his throne, congratulating himself on the swift administration of justice. Case closed.

Or is it? In what has to be the best one-liner in the Bible, the prickly prophet turns the tables and passes judgment on the judge. "You are the man!" rasps Nathan, and proceeds to point out the ways in which David has offended all of God's finer instincts. The "incident" with Uriah the Hittite had not gone unnoticed after all (see 2 Sam. 11). Had David seriously expected that it would? Had he thought that God would overlook his "appropriation" of Uriah's wife, Bathsheba? Or his subsequent "termination" of Uriah? David could describe his actions in whatever way he wished, but God was neither fooled nor mocked by his subterfuge. Murder, as they say, will out.

To David's credit, he does not deny his guilt. "I have sinned against the LORD," he admits bluntly (v. 13). Whatever blinders he had worn to shield himself from the appalling nature of his actions have fallen away. Perhaps Nathan's parable opened his eyes, giving him a quick and unforgiving glimpse of himself as others—and God—must see him.

David's heart must have frozen as he awaited sentencing. Would God's judgment be as swift and brutal as his own had been?

Nathan intones God's sentence in vv. 13 and 14—swift, certainly, but marginally more merciful. David himself would be spared, but the child born of his illicit union with Bathsheba would die.

Modern readers recoil at this verdict almost as much as David must have. What kind of justice, we ask, condemns the innocent to punish the guilty? Though I may appear to be sidestepping a legitimate and important theological issue, I would point out that the Bible itself does not seem concerned with this question. Scripture simply goes on to describe the awful after-effects of the sentence. For what it is worth—and it is surely worth something—God's judgment exacts an awful price on the now-penitent David.

Rather than embarking on the dangerous prospect of passing judgment on God, we might do better to consider the psychology of David's self-deception.

British Christian educator John Hall points out that David's self-deception was so complete that he did not even recognize himself when he was confronted with a similar story of ruthless selfishness. He had, evidently, reconstructed his own memory in such a way that his own sin did not loom so large. His self-deception had probably happened bit by bit—a rationalization here, a rationalization there—until finally he had a version of the story he could live with. If Nathan had never confronted him with a different and less flattering version of the facts, he might never have looked his own sin full in the face.

Two things strike me about this aspect of the story. The first is how easily we reconstruct reality to suit our own vanity. David's story reminds us that even the hearts of believers can be "deceitful above all things, and desperately wicked" (Jer. 17:9, KJV). Second, however, is the importance of checking our own version of reality against someone else's, preferably someone of considerable spiritual maturity. Do that person's perceptions bear any resemblance to our own?

Repentance is a critical part of life after grace, yet we cannot repent properly if we are caught in the snares of our own self-deception. Typically, one of two things happens when we are confronted with a sin about which we have deceived ourselves. Either we see the sin and respond with horror and repentance, or we dig our heels in deeper, denying a version of ourselves we cannot face. The first reaction is the first step toward forgiveness and wholeness. The second reaction is a recipe for spiritual disaster.

David, of course, chose the first. His repentance gave birth to a prayer than has helped generations of the faithful acknowledge their guilt and receive God's assurance of pardon. "The sacrifice acceptable to God is a broken spirit," he reminds us; "a broken and contrite heart, O God, you will not despise" (Ps. 51:17). He knew his subject well.

So does George Macdonald in these lines from his poem "A Fool I Bring," which seems designed for those of us struggling against self-deception. "With self, O Father, leave me not alone," he writes. "Leave not the beguiler with the beguiled; Besmirched and ragged, Lord, take back thine own. A fool I bring thee to be made a child."

For Reflection

1. Do you have anyone in your life who can confront you with your sin? How would/do you respond?
2. What would be necessary to change you from a "fool" to a "child"?
3. Write a recipe for spiritual disaster based on this story.

Hymn Suggestions

Various settings of Psalm 51 (GC 55, 56, 57; HPSS
195; NCH 186, 188; PsH 51; RIL 438; SNC 49, 50;
cf. SNC 51–59)

"My Faith Looks Up to Thee" (CH 576; H 691; HPSS
383; RIL 446; UMH 452)

"Today Your Mercy Calls Us" (LBW 304)

A Labor of Love

Luke 22:1–27

A labor and delivery nurse once told me of her experience working in a Catholic hospital. Opinion was apparently divided about the presence of the crucifix in the hospital's labor and delivery rooms. Officially, of course, no disagreement existed, but the laboring women formed no consensus whatsoever. Some women insisted on the crucifix's removal; others could not take their eyes from it. Yet, their difference of opinion was not along religious lines. Many women in the first group explained their aversion on the grounds that they wanted nothing more to do with men—human or divine. The second group, however, saw the crucifix as a significant source of comfort.

For people who doubt the plausibility of any level of serious reflection during labor and delivery, let me testify to the fact that it can and does happen. Knowing, I suppose, what an unparalleled opportunity this moment would afford (!), God gave me ample time for deliberation during the births of my two children. Though I had no crucifix on which to focus, my mind's eye was fixed firmly on a suffering savior. Truth to tell, the fact of that suffering enabled me to have any patience with God whatsoever. Who, after all, would want a God who could sit stoically by with no firsthand knowledge of human suffering?

Emily Dickinson once wrote, "When Jesus tells us about his Father, we distrust him. When he shows us his Home, we turn away, but when he confides to us that he is 'acquainted with Grief,' we listen, for that is also an Acquaintance of our own."

Were any women present in the upper room, I wonder? If so, let me venture to guess that they might not have been as clueless as the disciples seem to be in this story of Jesus' Last Supper. Jesus speaks openly of suffering here, breaking the bread of his body and pouring out the wine of his blood. Could anyone have missed such ominous clues as to what was coming? Could anyone have wondered what he meant when he commanded them to "Do this in remembrance of me"?

Yet, some of the disciples do miss his meaning. Hearing only what they want to hear, they immediately start to squabble about who will be the most indispensable in the coming kingdom. Their stupidity could only have compounded Jesus' suffering, yet he patiently explains that the leader in his kingdom must be servant of all.

This "suffering servant" language should not have been a surprise to anyone. Jesus began his ministry, after all, by reading the words of Isaiah's suffering servant and applying them to himself. (Compare Isa. 61:1–2 and 58:6 with Luke 4:16–21.) Still, perhaps no one could have guessed how radically Jesus would fulfill Isaiah's words about one who was "wounded for our transgressions, crushed for our iniquities." No one could have imagined the ways in which his punishment would make us whole, or how we would be healed by his bruises (see Isa. 53).

Arguing about whether women or men would have understood Jesus' words better is absurd, of course. To squabble over such things is to fall into the same fault as the disciples who argued about who would be the greatest. The important thing is that Jesus, knowing full well the foibles of those who gather round his table, looks us each in the eye and says, "I have eagerly desired to eat this Passover with you before I suffer" (Luke 22:15). Because he does, we can face our own suffering with renewed courage. With the "man of sorrows" at our side, we can be sure that our God does not just sympathize with our suffering, but actually experiences it with us—and for us. Even in the midst of life's most agonizing moments, we can be sure that "there is no place where earth's sorrows are more felt than up in heaven" (from "There's a Wideness in God's Mercy," by Frederick William Faber, 1854).

For Reflection

1. If God is so sympathetic about human suffering, why does God allow it to go on?
2. What are the risks of trying to answer question #1 with too much certainty?
3. What are the risks of not asking question #1 at all?

Hymn Suggestions

"There's a Wideness in God's Mercy" (CH 73; GC 626; H 469, 470; HPSS 298; RIL 349)

"Abide with Me" (CH 636; H 662; HPSS 543; LBW 272; NCH 99; PsH 442; RIL 440; UMH 700)

"We Cannot Measure How You Heal" (GC 575; SNC 69)

Grow Up in Grace

Ephesians 4:1–16

*H*annah spent the first year of her life in an orphanage. It was not as if she lived in squalor; the people who ran the orphanage did the best that they could with very limited resources. She and the other twelve babies were fed and changed regularly. The room where they stayed was warm and dry. Each baby had his or her own crib.

Yet, when Hannah first met her adoptive parents, they were dismayed by what they saw. The back of her head was flattened and bald. She could not crawl or talk. Her face had a dull, lifeless look. Hannah had apparently spent much of her first year lying on her back in her crib. As a result, she was way behind developmentally. Her new parents wondered if it was too late for her to catch up.

It was not too late, as it turned out. Hannah is now a happy, active child with an impish sense of humor and sparkling brown eyes. Yet her parents had no guarantee of a happy ending. Hannah's father tells of the surge of hope they felt when Hannah reached eagerly for a bunch of brightly colored plastic keys that they had brought along for that first meeting. He also tells about the frantic concern and growing frustration that they felt in the ensuing months as they cut through the rolls of red tape that prevented them from bringing Hannah home. They knew that Hannah was in desperate need of exercise, stimulation, and love. They also knew that every day in the orphanage was one more day that her brain, her body, and her spirit would atrophy.

We can sense the same kind of frustration in Ephesians 4. Paul pleads with the young Christians who are reading his letter to "grow up" in faith. He has just spent three chapters reminding them of the miracle of their adoption into the family of faith. The old life cannot hold a candle to the new. Yet now is no time to sit back and relax. New Christians need nourishment, exercise, stimulation, and love if they are ever going to "grow up in every way into him who is the head, into Christ" (v. 15).

Though Paul is obviously concerned about these baby Christians as individuals, he also has the broader church in mind. The "body" that concerns him the most is the body of Christ, which cannot function properly if individual parts are weak and undernourished.

Like the loving father in faith that he is, Paul sets out to lavish these little ones with what they need most. For nourishment, he prescribes a steady diet of humility, gentleness, and patience (v. 2). They will need all of these if they are to "maintain the unity of the Spirit in the bond of peace" (v. 3). Unity, evidently, cannot be attained passively. Neither is it optional, given the urgency with which Paul writes about it. What Olympic athlete, after all, could hope to compete without all the parts of his or her body striving toward the same goal?

Not surprisingly, exercise is Paul's next concern. Each individual Christian has been given gifts, which are not much good, however, if they are not developed. Drawing again upon our Olympic athlete analogy, what figure skater ever arrived at the medal platform without thousands of hours working out on the ice? Similarly, Paul urges his readers to commit themselves to a rigorous regimen of body building, remembering again that the body we are building is, in fact, the body of Christ (v. 12).

Without the kind of care and stimulation that Paul describes, the body cannot grow up healthy and strong, yet why do we so often act as if it can? Many adult Christians are little more than toddlers in terms of their faith development. We pay little attention to prayer; we rarely read the Bible. We send our kids off to Sunday school and act as if *we* have nothing more to learn. We indulge in fits of pride, prejudice, and temper instead of disciplining ourselves to the tougher tasks of humility, gentleness, and patience.

Paul pleads with all of us—no matter what our "age" in the faith—to keep building up the body of Christ. His urgency is born of a parent's desperation. We have been saved "by grace . . . through faith" (Eph. 2:8). But if we don't act fast, our faith may atrophy beyond the reach of restoration. To put the matter bluntly: We've been born again. Now we may need to grow up.

For Reflection

1. How would you characterize your "age" in the faith? For instance, are you an adolescent? a toddler? in a midlife crisis?
2. What areas of your faith have atrophied? What would be required to start them growing again?
3. Does your church emphasize being born again (conversion) or growing up in faith (sanctification)? What are the risks of doing one without the other?

Hymn Suggestions

"Take My Life and Let It Be" (CH 609; HPSS 391; LBW 406; PsH 288; NCH 448; RIL 475; UMH 399)
"Day By Day" (CH 599; H 645)
"Take This Moment" (GC 673)
"My Friends May You Grow in Grace" (SNC 288)
"All Who Believe and are Baptized" (H 298)

Close Encounters

Winner Take All

Romans 12:1

*I*t was part of the deal. Guests at the convent were to leave their rooms as they found them, ready for the next wayfaring stranger.

I dutifully opened the dresser drawer in search of clean sheets. I found them, along with a faded index card on which was printed the following prayer:

> O Lord, guide my hands as I make this bed ready for another's rest. May I be reminded that you prepared a lowly manger for a sleeping place, and make me aware of the importance and privilege of serving others in common places and everyday tasks. Help me perform this act with care and love, and may the one who follows me here be refreshed in body, mind and spirit. Amen.

Making a bed had never been such a spiritual experience. That simple act started me thinking about the extent to which God wants to be a part of our lives, right down to the most mundane activities.

The Old Testament certainly has a sense for this. In Deuteronomy 28, the list of covenant blessings includes, "Blessed shall be your basket and your kneading bowl" (v. 5). Back in the days before Wonder Bread, the kneading bowl must have been one of the most reliable facets of the daily routine. Yet God, apparently, has an eye for details; according to this passage, no detail is too small or too tedious to escape being bathed in blessing.

Perhaps this concept was in the back of the apostle Paul's mind when he appealed to us "to present your bodies as a living sacrifice" (Rom. 12:1). Unlike the "whole burnt offerings" of the Old Testament, Christians are called to be walking, talking sacrifices, offering the whole of our lives to God's service and glory.

This news, of course, is troubling for those of us who like to keep this "God thing" in manageable form. Heaven forbid that God should start creeping around our daily planner, infiltrating the whole of our lives instead of staying safely sequestered on Sunday mornings. Bed-making prayers might be fine for nuns, but isn't that kind of thing a little "over the top" for the rest of us?

Not according to Paul. Notice first that he makes no distinctions as to different levels of devotion, as if believers could be categorized as first- or second-class Christians. His appeal goes out to all of us equally.

Second, a very large "therefore" in this verse forms the basis for his audacious appeal. "I appeal to you *therefore,* brothers and sisters, by the mercies of God, to present your bodies as a living sacrifice, holy and acceptable to God, which is your spiritual worship" (italics added). For a full sense of the "therefore," we would have to read all of Romans 1–11, but perhaps the first two verses will suffice to summarize it all. Romans 8:1–2 says: "There is therefore now no condemnation for those who are in Christ Jesus. For the law of the Spirit of life in Christ Jesus has set you free from the law of sin and of death." In other words, our freedom has been bought with a price, won at the cost of Christ's own blood. Paul is simply reminding us that "winner takes all."

When viewed this way, Paul's appeal seems suddenly reasonable. In fact, "reasonable" is one way to translate the word at the end of Romans 12:1 that is often translated "spiritual" (". . . present your bodies as a living sacrifice, holy and acceptable to God, which is your *spiritual/reasonable* worship). The Greek word is *logiken*, a close cousin to our English word, "logic." And what, after all, could be more logical? If God has paid it all, why shouldn't we give it all? As the hymn writer says, "Love so amazing, so divine, demands my soul, my life, my all" (Isaac Watts, "When I Survey the Wondrous Cross").

Yet framing Paul's appeal only in terms of duty would be a shame. At least, we need to make sure that "duty" is not seen in a negative way. While giving God thanks at all times and in all places is appropriate, as one traditional communion liturgy reminds us, the task is a "joyful duty." Whether in the board room or the bedroom, on the tractor or at the table, God yearns to have a "close encounter" with us, to bathe every aspect of our lives in blessing. What could be better?

Think about it the next time you make the bed, and whisper yet one more line from Isaac Watts: "May all my work be praise" (from "My Shepherd Will Supply My Need").

For Reflection

1. To what degree has God infiltrated your daily life?
2. How might it change your attitude toward your day if you saw it as a living sacrifice?
3. What areas of your life most need to be bathed in prayer?

Hymn Suggestions

"When I Survey the Wondrous Cross" (CH 195; H 474; HPSS 100, 101; LBW 482; NCH 224; PsH 384; RIL 292, 293; UMH 298, 299)

"Alas! And Did My Savior Bleed" (CH 204; HPSS 78;
    LBW 98; NCH 199, 200; PsH 385; UMH 359, 294)
"Teach Me, My God and King" (H 592)
"All That We Have" (GC 601; cf. SNC 218)

Call Waiting

1 Samuel 3:1–20

*P*eople usually do not expect the Bible to be funny. But just try to read 1 Samuel 3 without smiling.

Young Samuel is settling in for the night. He hears a voice calling his name and assumes that the voice belongs to the elderly priest, Eli. An obedient kid, Samuel is at Eli's side in a flash with the words, "Here I am, for you called me." But surprise. Eli doesn't know what Samuel is talking about and tells the boy to go back to bed. Samuel does as he is told, only to have the exact same thing happen. Just as he gets his pillow fluffed and his blanket pulled up around his chin, the voice calls again, "Samuel, Samuel."

We do not know if Samuel is annoyed. The Bible only tells us that he gets up and goes again to the old man's bedside. We can only imagine that his voice might be tinged with impatience as he repeats the exact same words, "Here I am, *for you called me*" (italics added).

Let's pause for a moment to take stock of the dynamics here. Anyone who has children or who has ever been a child (that's pretty much everyone) is familiar with the "jumping-bean syndrome" in children's bedtime rituals. Just as the parent sits down for a well-deserved moment of peace and privacy, the supposedly sleeping child appears with some real or imagined concern that requires the parent's immediate attention. The parent is patient the first time and perhaps, by reason of strength, for the second. But by third time the pitter-patter of little feet is heard on the stairs . . . well, let's just say the excuse had better be good.

From Eli's perspective, Samuel's behavior must have looked like a clear case of the jumping-bean syndrome. We can imagine his words, "I did not call, my son; lie down again," inflected with a tad more tension each time as well. Yet, think for a moment how all of this seems to the otherwise obedient Samuel. He knows it's not the jumping-bean thing, and yet, somebody seems to be setting him up to take the rap for it.

We smile because we see their mutual misunderstanding unfolding before us. We smile because we've all been there/ done that with the jumping-bean syndrome. Finally we smile, because we know something the characters don't. We know, thanks to what the narrator has told us in v. 4, that the Lord and not Eli is calling Samuel's name.

Even though Eli's eyes had begun to grow dim (v. 2), he sees just enough to discern the shape of what is going on in verse 8. When Samuel shows up at Eli's side for the third time, Eli perceives that God is the one calling the boy. He tells him to go and lie down again, but if he hears his name again, to say, "Speak, LORD, for your servant is listening."

Now that the readers and the characters are all on the same page, humor steps aside for something more serious. When God calls again, the news is so scathing that it "will make both ears of anyone who hears of it tingle" (v. 11).

Much more could be said about the content of this oracle and the human characters' response to it. But let's focus on the way God's call comes to Samuel. God's call comes in the midst of confusion in this story. First, we see the comic confusion of the jumping-bean syndrome. There is something heartening, I think, about the fact that God sometimes chooses to speak to us through the comic confusion of everyday life. At the very least, God seems to have a sense of humor.

Second, there is confusion at the level of leadership. God's call comes with the help of a half-blind priest. Sight is almost always symbolic in the Bible, and here it certainly is. Eli's eyes are no longer reliable; he does not see God clearly anymore. Yet God uses his partial sight to point Samuel and the people of God to a clearer vision of the covenant. Something is reassuring here for both leaders and those people who are led.

Finally, there is confusion about what God wants. God's call interrupts an already existing call. Samuel thinks he is all set. He is apprenticed to a priest, well on his way to a promising career. His life has already been dedicated to God, after all. What more could God want of him? Yet, God does want something more . . . something else. In this passage, God interrupts Samuel's plans with an ancient version of "call waiting."

Could God be calling your name somehow in this passage? God seems to be willing to call as many times as it takes. Still, maybe the time has come for you to pay attention to that click on the line of your life's confusion. You might just have a call waiting.

For Reflection

1. Do you relate more strongly to Eli or to Samuel in this story? Why?
2. Can you think of a time when God called to you during a time of confusion?
3. How do we tell the difference between God's voice and our own?

Hymn Suggestions

"How Clear Is Our Vocation, Lord" (HPSS 419; RIL 433)

"Here I Am, Lord" (CH 452; GC 686; HPSS 525; SNC
    268; UMH 593)
"Jesus Calls Us" (CH 337; H 550; LBW 494; NCH 171,
    172; PsH 553; RIL 258, 259; UMH 398)
"Will You Come and Follow Me" (SNC 267)

A View from the Balcony

Ecclesiastes 3:1–14

*B*etween the two of them, they could quote the whole poem.

> Nature's first green is gold,
> Her hardest hue to hold.
> Her early leaf's a flower;
> But only so an hour.
> Then leaf subsides to leaf.
> So Eden sank to grief,
> So dawn goes down to day.
> Nothing gold can stay.

The poem was by Robert Frost. The setting was a balcony in the Blue Ridge Mountains. The season was spring, or more specifically, those first fleeting days of spring when the trees sport tassels of what the Crayola Company calls "green yellow." Frost's description is, of course, more telling because it hints at value as well as hue.

The couple quoting the poem had a keen sense of both the beauty and the worth of nature's first green gold. The couple did not necessarily embody the energy and promise of spring; in fact, their faces spoke more eloquently of fall. Yet, perhaps because their lives were in a later season, they could appreciate the poignancy of the poem. Try telling a teenager that "nothing gold can stay." Life and loss are the only true teachers of that lesson.

The author of Ecclesiastes (in Hebrew, simply "the Preacher") would have been very much at home on that balcony. His own poetry conveys some of the same sense of time's relentless progression. Yet the Preacher's poem is suffused with a sense of the rightness and appropriateness of that progression. "For everything there is a season," he writes, "and a time for every matter under heaven" (Eccl. 3:1).

As we look down the litany of timely matters in verses 2–8, we are tempted to accentuate the positive and eliminate the negative. We have more fun, after all, laughing, dancing, and embracing than weeping, mourning, and not embracing. The Preacher knows, however, that timing is everything. Weeping and mourning are appropriate at a graveside in a way that laughing and dancing are not. A passionate embrace fits far better in a bedroom than a boardroom. Even birth and death have their day. Anyone who has sat by the bed of a dying saint, for instance, can appreciate the wisdom of Job's question, "Why is light given to one in misery, and life to the bitter in soul, who long for death, but it does not come . . . ?" (Job 3:20–21a). At certain times, death can indeed be a "consummation devoutly to be wished."

One of the things that wisdom teaches is the ability to discern the signs of such times and to act accordingly. Yet even the wise run up against the limits of human understanding. Confessing that God "has made everything suitable for its time" (Eccl. 3:11) is one thing, but claiming that we understand how and why is quite another. This mystery forms the crux of the rest of verse 11 and, for that matter, the human predicament. While God "has put a sense of past and future into [our] minds, yet [we] cannot find out what God has done from the beginning to the end."

The question is one of perspective. Made in God's own image, we are close enough to God to imagine a grand design, but too close to the minutia of our own day-to-day existence to see it. In everyday language, we cannot see the forest for the trees.

Once we have acknowledged our limits, the question then becomes, "How do we live life faithfully in the midst of those limits?" The Preacher has some words of wisdom on that score as well. First, he urges us to get up on the balcony—to make use of our limited human perspective to see as much of the forest as we can. The wise, he implies, try hard to discern the right action and attitude for all of life's situations. This activity, in a sense, is part of "the business that God has given to everyone to be busy with" (v. 10).

Once we have made this step, however, the Preacher urges us to let go—to relax—to "eat and drink and take pleasure in all [our] toil" (v. 13). "I know," he tells us in verse 12, "that there is nothing better for [humans] than to be happy and enjoy themselves as long as they live."

Far from being a call to hedonism, these words urge us to a life of awe, responsibility, and trust. This is what the "balcony couple" at the beginning of this Bible study embodied. A retired missionary couple, they had worked hard to live lives of faithfulness and discernment. Now, sitting comfortably beside each other, eating ice cream with friends, they looked out over the green-gold mountain grandeur and savored the glory of spring without any bitterness about its brevity. Facing the onset of their own personal fall, they seemed content to confess that "for everything there is a season" (Eccl. 3:1).

For Reflection

1. How does our culture's call to "go for all the gusto you can get" differ from Ecclesiastes' call to eat, drink, and be merry?
2. Are you as content as that couple on the balcony? Why or why not?

3. What season are you in? How has that affected your perspective on the Christian life?

Hymn Suggestions

"God of Our Life" (CH 713; HPSS 275; NCH 366; RIL 58, 59)

"Now Thank We All Our God" (GC 565; CH 715; H 396, 397; HPSS 555; LBW 533, 534; NCH 419; PsH 454; RIL 61; UMH 102)

"Amen, siakudu misa" (SNC 287)

In Your Dreams

Acts 12:1–17

*H*ave you ever lived a nightmare? Have you ever been in a situation so horrific that you would have given anything to wake up and discover it was all a dream?

Welcome to the apostle Peter's worst nightmare.

What must it have been like to fall asleep flanked by two guards? How does one get comfortable in a tangle of chains?

In actuality, chains and guards were the least of Peter's problems. More pressing was the fact that he was scheduled to appear before Herod the next morning. This same Herod had put to death the apostle James just a few days before. Herod and the crowds had tasted blood and liked it, a fact that did not bode well for Peter the following day.

As Peter settled in for what could well be his final night, one has to wonder what was on his mind. Did the guards taunt him about his prospects? Did he picture the rest of the believers at prayer (v. 5), or did he simply feel forgotten? Did he think about the fact that it was the last night of Passover? As he closed his eyes that night, did he wonder whether God would deliver him as God had delivered the Israelites at that first Passover long ago (Exod. 12:21ff.)? Or did he simply taste the bitter irony of being behind bars on the night when everyone he loved was celebrating freedom?

With reality such a nightmare, sleep must have offered a welcome, if fitful, escape. Small wonder that when the angel showed up in a shower of light Peter should assume he was

49

dreaming. He'd had visions before, after all (see Acts 10:9ff.). Maybe this sort of thing happened every time he went to bed hungry. . . .

The poke in the ribs felt real enough, though, and this angel seemed to have a surprisingly practical streak. When the chains fell off (!), the angel matter-of-factly ordered Peter to fasten his belt and put on his sandals. Next came the order to button up his overcoat. (Was it a disguise or just chilly?) Peter must have smiled to himself. This dream was becoming better and better! The two set off—out of the cell, past the guards, and to the iron gates that led to the city. The gates parted just like Peter's own personal Red Sea, and they walked through to freedom. Wow, this dream was the best he'd ever had!

Suddenly, Peter found himself standing alone in an alley. Chills that had nothing to do with the temperature swept over his skin. The angel was nowhere to be seen, and he realized with a jolt that he was very much awake. But if he was awake, the guards might well be, too. Muttering a prayer of thanksgiving under his breath, he made for the house of Mary, the mother of John Mark. Did he know that in this very place the believers had gathered to pray for him, or was this just another divine coincidence? Either way, God was clearly still guiding him—angel or no angel.

Peter's welcome was almost comic. Did he knock softly at first, so as not to attract attention? Did he have to increase the urgency of the knock to attract the believers' attention? Perhaps they were reluctant to interrupt their prayer meeting, and so sent young Rhoda to answer the door.

To say that she was surprised at the identity of the visitor would be something of an understatement. Imagine Peter's frustration (and fear?) as the overjoyed Rhoda ran back to tell the believers that Peter had come to call, meanwhile forgetting to let him in off the street! When she does announce the news, they look up from their prayers only long enough to say, in essence, "In your dreams, Rhoda."

God doesn't always consider perfect faith a prerequisite for answered prayers, which is a good thing. The perpetual surprise of both Peter and the rest of the believers in this story makes this point clear. They did not really expect God to deliver Peter, at least not in this life. Somehow, they never imagined that God could walk into their worst nightmare and turn it into a reality far better than their fondest dreams.

We must be careful when we read stories like this not to conclude that life always ends "happily ever after" for Christians. Peter, after all, lived to preach another day in this story, but later ended up a martyr. Still, this story alerts us to the fact that God can and often does do far more than we ask or think. We should certainly think about that fact as we settle in for the night in our prison cell. Could God be waiting to break into your worst nightmare? Tomorrow at this time, could your chains be lying empty on the ground?

For Reflection

1. What is your worst nightmare? Do you have room for God in it?
2. Has God ever answered your prayers in ways that surprised you?
3. How might God use you to liberate others?

Hymn Suggestions

"Precious Lord, Take My Hand" (CH 628; GC 874; HPSS 404: NCH 472; PsH 493; UMH 474))
"I Love the Lord, Who Heard My Cry" (HPSS 362; NCH 511; SNC 226, 227)
"You That Know the Lord Is Gracious" (RIL 424)
"Alleluia! Sing to Jesus" (H 461; HPSS 144; LBW 158; NCH 257; PsH 406; RIL 346)

When God Steps Off the Screen

Luke 4:14–30

*S*everal years ago, Woody Allen wrote and directed a movie called *The Purple Rose of Cairo*. It tells the story of a woman who goes to the movies every day. She is trying to escape from the dullness and despair of her own life, and she appears to be succeeding. The movie theater has become her world, her reality. The characters are her closest companions. She is so intimate with their dialogue that her lips move right along with their lines. But one day, something strange happens.

Right in the middle of a perfectly predictable scene, one of the characters makes a radical departure from the script. He does a double take, squints out into the darkened theater, and looks directly at the woman. "You must really love this picture," he says. "You've been here all day, and I've seen you here twice before!"

She is flabbergasted, of course. This isn't supposed to happen. Suddenly, the dialogue she knows by heart is all wrong. Now she has to think of something to say. But as she sits struggling for words, the truly unthinkable happens: the character actually steps off the screen. People around her start screaming and fainting. In technical terms, the proscenium—that imaginary plane that separates the stage from the audience—is hopelessly broken. In personal terms, the borders of this woman's reality are impossibly blurred. Nothing will ever be the same.

It must have felt a bit like this in the synagogue in Nazareth for those who had eyes to see and ears to hear. What happened that day in Nazareth was no less a miracle, after all. Jesus stepped off the scroll, and the borders of the world's reality have never been the same.

Yet few people seem to have understood the significance of what they'd witnessed when Jesus rolled up the Isaiah scroll and announced, "Today this scripture has been fulfilled in your hearing." Instead of a sharp intake of breath, we hear only self-satisfied murmurs. "Hey, how about that carpenter's kid? Quite the gift for public speaking!" Perhaps the judges at the back of Jesus' hometown synagogue held up their scorecards: 9.7; 9.8; 9.7; 9.9. . . .

No wonder Jesus was furious. The Word made flesh had spoken in their hearing, and they were treating it like a speech contest! But he refused to go along with it, and proceeded to do something you'd never do at a speech contest. He intentionally irritated—yea, infuriated—his audience. Jesus turned the Scripture's own stories on them like a mirror and showed them the worst side of themselves. They didn't like what they saw, so they ran him out of town by way of a convenient cliff.

What were those stories, and why did they make the people so angry? In short, they were stories about God's extravagant grace. In the first, God's grace spills over to a Sidonian widow and her son at the brink of starvation (1 Kgs. 17:1, 8–16). In the second, a Syrian general is cured of leprosy (2 Kgs. 5:1–14). Though these stories seem harmless enough at first glance, they suggest something downright scandalous: insiders do not have a corner on the market of God's grace. In a sense, Jesus' use of these two stories is a kind of ultimatum, as if he is saying, "Look, if you don't have the wit to see that I am the fulfillment of Isaiah's prophecy, then I'll take the good news to someone who does!"

We could easily turn smug at this point and shake our heads about why "those Jews" just didn't seem to get it. Before we grow too complacent, however, we should remember that these people were part of the religious establishment. Regular churchgoers, you might say. As a regular churchgoer myself, I have to admit that I am not immune to the occasional bout of blindness. How many times, I wonder, does Jesus step off the screen on a given Sunday morning without our taking any notice? Often we are too dazzled by how we're doing to see him. We are too deafened by our own eloquence to hear him. We are almost certainly too preoccupied to have a genuine conversation with him.

Christmas is the time of year when we celebrate the Word becoming flesh and dwelling among us. The unrepeatable fact of the incarnation was God's way of stepping off the screen. At the very least, we ought to recognize the wonder of that electrifying moment. Yet, in a certain sense, God continues to come among us—both to comfort and confront. Be alert for such moments as you move through the coming days. Perhaps it will happen during a perfectly predictable hymn or a Scripture reading. Maybe the moment will occur as you notice the tears in your neighbor's eyes. However it happens, know that Jesus is doing a double take. He is staring out into the darkened world and looking straight at you. What will you say? What will you do?

For Reflection

1. In what ways has God stepped off the screen for you lately?
2. When you meet Jesus' eyes, do you see comfort or confrontation?
3. What will you say? What will you do?

Hymn Suggestions

"O Lord, How Shall I Meet You?" (HPSS 11; LBW 23; PsH 331; RIL 368)

"Bring We the Frankincense of Our Love" (HPSS 62)
"Be Thou My Vision" (CH 595; H 488; HPSS 339; RIL
  67; UMH 451)
"I Heard the Voice of Jesus Say" (GC 646; H 692; LBW
  497; NCH 489; PsH 488)
"Will You Come and Follow Me?" (SNC 267)

The Thing with Feathers

Ruth 2:17–23

*C*an you imagine leftovers giving you a new lease on life? Difficult as this is to comprehend, it is precisely what happens in this passage.

Before her daughter-in-law Ruth shows up with nearly a bushel of barley and leftovers from lunch, Naomi is at the brink of despair. Her husband and two grown sons are dead, and she seems inclined to join them. Her bitterness boils over earlier in the book when her friends rush to welcome her home after more than a decade away. Hearing her name on their lips she snaps, "Call me no longer Naomi ['Pleasant']. Call me Mara ['Bitter'], for the Almighty has dealt bitterly with me. I went away full, but the LORD has brought me back empty" (1:20–21).

Well, not *quite* empty. In her acrid outburst, Naomi has overlooked her single most valuable asset: Ruth.

In the eyes of ancient Israelite culture, of course, Ruth must have looked more like a liability. Ruth was a foreigner and thus suspect on the basis of both her nationality and her religion. There was reason to suspect she was barren, given that she had not produced a child during her ten years of marriage to Naomi's son (1:4–5). (Infertility was blamed on the woman in those days.) With no reasonable chance of marriage, Ruth must have seemed like dead weight around the neck of a woman who was already downwardly mobile.

This pessimistic assessment does not take into account God's standards of measurement, however. Ruth rates high in a quality that is most often attributed to God: steadfast love. In older translations, it is sometimes called "lovingkindness." By any name it is love that goes above and beyond the call of duty. Ruth shows this love when, in spite of Naomi's orders to return to the security of her own parents, Ruth clings, terrier-like, to her mother-in-law. "Do not press me to leave you or to turn back from following you!" she insists in 1:16. "Where you go, I will go; where you lodge, I will lodge; your people shall be my people, and your God my God. Where you die, I will die—there will I be buried." Ruth's decision could well have led to a double plot in Bethlehem's cemetery. Yet, God seems to have had other ideas.

While Naomi is content to sit home and wait for the grim reaper, Ruth wakes up early and goes out to glean. As luck—or Providence—would have it, she ends up in the field of Naomi's relative. Cousin Boaz notices Ruth right away and wastes no time issuing orders designed to guarantee both her safety and her success.

Thus, the leftovers. When Ruth returns from the field that day, she's clearly made a real haul. Naomi is quick to ask, "Where did you glean today?" When Ruth reveals the name of their benefactor, Naomi comes back to life. "Blessed be he by the LORD," she exclaims, "whose kindness [steadfast love] has not forsaken the living or the dead!"

This outburst presents quite a contrast to her earlier one, which was so full of bitterness and blame. "What happened?" we may well ask. If you've ever experienced an ounce of Naomi's bitterness, if you've ever shared a fraction of her despair, if you've ever entertained even for a moment the urge to shake your fist at God, then you're going to want to know the answer to that question. *What happened?*

In a word, hope happened. And hope, as Emily Dickinson tells us, is

. . . the thing with feathers
That perches in the soul—
And sings the tune without the words—
And never stops—at all.

Why do I love that poem? Let me count the ways. First, I love it because it recognizes that hope is not some flimsy, ephemeral fantasy that we conjure up to make ourselves feel better. Hope is not something that we manufacture by thinking good thoughts or praying polite prayers. Hope is not the brave face we put on at the funeral home or the lawyer's office. Hope is a tangible—albeit small—thing that flaps in fresh from its permanent perch at God's altars and makes its nest right smack in the middle of our despair. And hope sings and sings and sings until, at the very least, we start humming along.

If Naomi had been given to poetry, she might have put it this way:

Hope is the thing with fiber
That your daughter-in-law brings home—
It trains its tongue around a name—
That says—you're not alone.

OK, so she wasn't Emily Dickinson, but the idea is the same. Hope is tangible. The grain had been sent from God. So had Ruth. So had Boaz. And in that moment, Naomi knew it. Knowing it, she exchanged her accusations for a doxology.

What would it take for you to do the same?

For Reflection

1. Christian scholars across the centuries have suggested that coincidences may be God's way of remaining anonymous. Look for examples of "divine coincidences" in Ruth's story and your own.

2. Have you ever been as bitter as Naomi? Is that level of bitterness unfaithful to God? Why or why not?
3. What are the tangible signs of God's steadfast love in your life? in the life of the Church? in the life of the world?

Hymn Suggestions

"Now Thank We All Our God" (GC 565; CH 715; H 396, 397; HPSS 555; LBW 533, 534; NCH 419; PsH 454; RIL 61; UMH 102)

"Our God, Our Help in Ages Past" (CH 67; H 680; HPSS 210; LBW 320; NCH 25; PsH 170; RIL 1; UMH 117)

"We Cannot Measure How You Heal" (GC 575; SNC 69)

When Believers Disagree

Jeremiah 28

*W*hat happens when believers disagree? Tension mounts as each side defends its take on the truth. Both claim the Bible as the basis for their position. Feelings are hurt, friendships strained, and the body of Christ ends up battered and broken.

We don't have to go far to discover this scenario, unfortunately. Abortion, homosexuality, and genetic engineering put believers at odds every time someone dares to bring up the topics. Or perhaps we need go no farther than divorce court or the dinner table for compelling examples.

No, we don't lack examples. We lack guidance.

Some help may hail from an obscure passage in Jeremiah. The setting for Jeremiah 28 could not have been more explosive. Religion and politics were wound together to form the fuse that threatened to ignite and destroy all of God's promises to the covenant people. King Zedekiah of Judah was under a lot of pressure to defuse the situation by rebelling against Babylon and throwing off the "yoke" of oppression that Babylon's king had placed on the people of Judah. After all, Babylon had already taken captive many of the religious and civic leaders, and looted the temple of most of its treasures. The time was ripe for rebellion. Surely, the people of Judah could count on God to back their plans for battle.

Enter the prophet Hananiah with just the words Zedekiah was waiting to hear. "Thus says the LORD of hosts, the God of Israel," Hananiah proclaimed confidently.

Within two years I will bring back to this place all the ves-
sels of the LORD's house, which King Nebuchadnezzar of
Babylon took away from this place and carried to Babylon. I will also bring back to this place King Jeconiah . . .
of Judah, and all the exiles from Judah who went to Babylon, says the LORD, for I will break the yoke of the king of
Babylon. (vv. 2–4)

While the words may have been welcome to the king, they
were oddly jarring to the prophet Jeremiah. They went
against every word he'd had from the Lord lately. According
to the revelations he'd received, God had placed the Baby-
lonian "yoke" on the people as punishment for their infi-
delity. God had even ordered Jeremiah to wear an actual yoke
so that the prophet himself would serve as a walking
reminder of God's judgment (Jer. 27:2). Imagine Jeremiah's
dismay, then, when Hananiah announces the "good news."

"Let him have it!" we, the readers, root. But Jeremiah does
not. Instead, he seems to step meekly aside in the face of this
new word from the Lord. "Amen! May the LORD do so," he
says. "May the LORD fulfill the words that you have prophe-
sied" (28:6).

Now comes our turn to be dismayed. Has Jeremiah suddenly undergone a personality transplant? The key to his baf-
fling behavior is in what he says next. In words spiced with
both skepticism and sarcasm, he suggests that the only way
to tell who is right is to wait and see whose words come
true. It is a fairly simple litmus test for true and false
prophecy given in Deuteronomy 18:20–22. The only thing
required is patience.

This story may seem like a long way to go for guidance on
how to referee disputes between believers, but Jeremiah's
reaction is very telling. Until his words are vindicated by God
through history, or until he receives another word from the
Lord that contradicts Hananiah's, he cannot be sure whose
position is right. For all he knows, Hananiah may have a

genuine word from the Lord. In the meantime, Jeremiah is free only to argue his position and point out the probabilities. Even when his adversary resorts to humiliation and violence (Hananiah actually takes the yoke from Jeremiah's neck and breaks it), Jeremiah does not respond in kind. In what has to be one of the most frustrating phrases in Scripture, Jeremiah 28:11 says, "At this, the prophet Jeremiah went his way."

Most of us do not receive direct revelations from God in the same way that the Old Testament prophets did. Moreover, many of our disputes are not so neatly depicted in black and white. Yet something can be learned from Jeremiah's demeanor in this story. The next time we square off—especially with another believer—we would do well to remember Jeremiah's refusal to claim a corner on the truth. Who knows? God may be speaking to our adversary too. Until we know for sure, perhaps the best we can do is to argue our case and simply walk away. Truth—like murder—will out.

For Reflection

1. Think of disagreements you have had/are having with other believers. Does this story make you wish you had acted differently? How might it impact your own words and actions in the future?
2. What's the difference between humility and weakness?
3. When you disagree with another Christian (or group of them), do you seek avenues of reconciliation? What are some of the ways we can promote healing in the body of Christ even when we continue to disagree?

Hymn Suggestions

"Great God, Your Love Has Called Us Here" (HPSS 353; RIL 503; UMH 579)

"The Church's One Foundation" (CH 272; H 525;
    HPSS 442; LBW 369; NCH 386; PsH 502; RIL 394;
    UMH 545)
"The Broken Body" (GC 737)
"Lord, Make Us Servants" (H 593; SNC 204)
"Like the Murmur of a Dove's Song" (CH 245; H 513;
    HPSS 314; NCH 270; SNC 171; UMH 544)

The Calm after the Storm

Mark 4:35–41

*J*ames and John stared ruefully into their wine cups. Being brothers, they were used to companionable silences, but this wasn't one of them. They were still trying to puzzle out the events of the night before, and the silence hung sullenly between them. James finally blurted out, "I thought he was talking to us."

"What?" asked John, startled out of his stupor.

"I thought he was talking to us. You know. When he sat up and shouted, 'Peace! Be still!'"

"Ha!" barked his brother after a suitably stunned silence.

Heads turned, and curiosity stilled the conversations of the other seaside diners. James hissed, "Be quiet. I don't want to attract too much attention. Besides, it was a perfectly reasonable assumption. We'd just shaken him out of a sound sleep. And then you had to get all hysterical and accuse him of not caring that we were about to sink like a rock."

"I was *not* hysterical. And I *had* to shout to be heard over the wind. And we *were* about to sink like a rock."

"Hush!" hissed James again, trying to check his brother's temper with his own. They weren't called the "Sons of Thunder" for nothing.

"All right," conceded John more quietly. "I guess I did go a little overboard when I asked him whether he cared."

"I wish you wouldn't talk about going 'overboard,'"

teased James with just the suggestion of a smile. At last the tension between the two was stilled.

The waitress brought their fish and chips. After an appropriate blessing, they munched companionably for a few minutes before John continued with a question. "What was the scariest part for you?"

"Funny you should ask," mused James, pushing the crumbs around on his plate. "I know I've always had nightmares about drowning in a storm, but that wasn't actually the part that got to me the most. It was when I realized that he hadn't been shushing *us* at all. It was when everything went suddenly, deafeningly silent, and I looked around and realized that it was *the storm* he'd been shushing."

The hairs on the back of John's neck were standing at attention. "I know what you mean. That's exactly what I was thinking. What's scarier, after all—a storm at sea or someone who can calm the storm? With only a few words, no less!"

Both brothers were silent again. Finally James ventured, "What have we gotten ourselves into here?"

"Another good question, Brother," responded John. "This is the first time we've had a nice, quiet meal in weeks. We're traveling constantly. And sometimes I feel more like a bodyguard than a disciple."

"You've got that right," replied James. "The crowds are incredible . . . always pressing closer and closer. The only way to keep him from getting crushed is to put him in a boat just offshore. And sometimes I wonder whether that will protect him. It's amazing what people will do just to be near him."

At this comment they both smiled, realizing simultaneously that the observation could apply to them. They'd gone to considerable lengths to be near him, too.

"It was a fine career in fish management we had going for us," remarked John wryly. "Do you ever regret walking away from it?"

"Not 'regret' exactly. But I wonder a lot. Not just about whether we're right to keep following him, but about who in the world he really is." James paused for a moment before continuing in a hushed voice. "All day I've been remembering those verses from Psalm 89: 'O LORD God of hosts, who is as mighty as you? You rule the raging of the sea. . . .'"

"'. . . when its waves rise, you still them,'" John finished the quote for him. The two sat staring at each other for a while, neither daring to follow the connection to its impossible conclusion.

John cleared his throat abruptly and pushed back his chair.

"No. Wait," insisted James. "Who is he? What do you think, really?"

John answered vaguely, "I'm not sure. I'm not sure of anything these days, except that I'd follow him anywhere." Then he turned on his heel and walked toward the door.

"Trust John to leave me stuck with the bill," muttered James, throwing down a silver coin and rushing to catch up with his brother.

For Reflection

1. What did you notice about this story that you may not have noticed before?
2. What does Jesus' power over nature in this story imply? How do you think Jesus' contemporaries felt about those implications? How do those implications make you feel?
3. What for you is the hardest thing about following Jesus?

Hymn Suggestions

"O Master, Let Me Walk with Thee" (CH 602; H 659, 660; HPSS 357; LBW 492; PsH 573; RIL 428; UMH 430)

"Take Up Your Cross, the Savior Said" (GC 698; H 675; HPSS 393; LBW 398; NCH 204; RIL 268; UMH 415)

"Thuma Mina/Send Me Lord" (GC 677; NCH 360; SNC 280; UMH 497)

God at the Door

Revelation 3:14–22

We've all seen it. Perhaps on the wall of some Sunday school classroom that smelled of floor wax and Elmer's glue. Perhaps in your grandparents' parlor, hung reverently over the piano. Or maybe lost among a dozen Victorian paintings in a booth at the antique mall. But wherever we've seen William Holman Hunt's painting of Jesus knocking at the door, the image is a part of our culture's collective memory.

Back in the nineteenth century, many people would have recognized Hunt's painting as an allusion to Revelation 3:20: "Listen! I am standing at the door, knocking; if you hear my voice and open the door, I will come in to you and eat with you, and you with me." The invitation sounds so appealing, just as Hunt's painting appeals with its gentle Jesus, politely knocking at the vine-trimmed door. Still, the Jesus of Revelation is far more passionate than Hunt's painting implies. A look at the larger context of this verse suggests that Hunt might better have depicted Jesus with more anguish and less patience, knuckles bloodied by the force of his blows on an unyielding door.

The passage in question is the last of seven letters to be sent to the seven churches of Asia Minor. Most of the letters are a mix of encouragement and criticism. But Jesus' words to the church at Laodicea are particularly intense. Or perhaps they only seem so because they cut so close to the bone.

"I know your works," Jesus says in verse 15 and following. "You are neither cold nor hot. I wish that you were either cold or hot. So, because you are lukewarm, and neither cold nor hot, I am about to spit you out of my mouth."

So much for "gentle Jesus meek and mild." Yet this glimpse of a far less comforting Jesus still offers a backhanded kind of comfort. This Jesus cares deeply about us and is determined to jolt us out of our complacency. He sees right through our self-sufficiency. We may think we are rich, that we have prospered, that we need nothing (v. 17). But Jesus sees us as we are: "wretched, pitiable, poor, blind, and naked."

This approach, we may say to ourselves, is no way to win friends and influence people. Jesus would not go far as a seeker-sensitive preacher. Yet Jesus is not trying to win friends or converts here. He is pleading with people who already call themselves Christians. He is begging us "to lead a life worthy of the calling to which [we] have been called," both as individuals and the Church (Eph. 4:1). His disgust at our tepid temperature is only matched by the passion with which he tries to talk his way back into our hearts.

The God of the Bible is often significantly at variance with the God—or gods—of popular piety. A passage like this one offers us an important reality check. If we believe Jesus' claim that, "if you know me, you will know my Father" (John 14:7), then we will have to factor this passage into our picture of God.

A friend of mine once characterized life as "a dark ride through a dark universe." His cynicism was born of pain, I think. In his experience, God seemed distant at best, malevolent at worst. Yet the pleading, passionate Christ of this passage argues against both cynicism and despair, as well as against any misguided impression that God is as disinterested as we often are. God does care. God cares passionately. And if our sin grieves God to the heart (Gen. 6:6), then our pain surely does as well.

Hunt had one thing right in that old painting. No latch appears on the outside of the door. It has to be opened from the inside. Listen. Jesus is standing at the door knocking . . . knocking until his knuckles are bruised and bloodied. He's pleading with all the passion of God. What will it take for you to let him in?

For Reflection

1. What temperature are you as a Christian?
2. Have you kept God waiting outside any doors/areas of your life? What are they? Why is it so hard to let God in?
3. How does this passage affect your picture of God?

Hymn Suggestions

"Somebody's Knocking at Your Door" (GC 395; HPSS 382)

"Come Down, O Love Divine" (CH 582; GC 465; H 516; HPSS 313; LBW 508; NCH 289; RIL 444; UMH 475)

"I Sought the Lord, and Afterward I Knew" (H 689; PsH 498; UMH 341)

"Listen, God Is Calling" (SNC 65)

Surprised by Joy

2 Kings 4:8–17

I had a bad attitude that day as I slid into my customary pew in the seminary chapel. I had already heard seven student sermons that week, and it was only Wednesday. I wasn't sure I had the strength for another.

I should have been relieved, then, when the student who was slotted to lead that day's chapel service announced that he would not deliver a sermon. "Today," he announced enthusiastically, "we're going to have a healing service!"

My heart sank. Perhaps you are surprised that a seminary professor would have such a cynical response, but my feelings reflected not so much cynicism as weariness. It had been a difficult year . . . or more accurately, a difficult decade. In my battle-scarred state, I was inclined to become impatient with the simplistic way some of my young, fresh-faced students interpreted "Ask, and it will be given you" (Matt. 7:7).

Several "healing stations" were set up around the room. Each was equipped with a kneeling bench and a person ready to pray with us for whatever healing we might need. I assessed the options and walked resolutely to the station where I thought I might sustain the least amount of damage.

As I knelt down, the earnest young seminarian at this particular station asked me if I'd like to pray for anything special. I smiled at her, shook my head, and indicated that something generic would be fine.

I knew I was in trouble the moment she began. "Lord," she prayed, her hands gently enfolding my head, "we ask that you would give Carol JOY!" *No, no,* my mind objected. *You don't understand my situation. Pray for patience, or endurance. But not joy. Joy is clearly out of the question.* But she kept right on praying, each request more extravagant than the last. No matter how I raised my mental defenses, I could not seem to stem the exuberant tide.

We see the Shunammite woman in 2 Kings 4 taking much the same psychological stance. The prophet Elisha has just offered her what she wants most in the world: a son. Yet, she mentally raises her arms as if to fend off the blessing. "No, my lord, O man of God; do not deceive your servant."

We can't help but admire her for it. Her response indicates that her hospitality toward the itinerant prophet has not been for anything she might get out of it. When she convinced her elderly husband to remodel their house to accommodate Elisha and his servant, her actions must have been purely out of the goodness of her heart. That she went above and beyond the call of duty is obvious from Elisha's reference to her taking "all this trouble for us" (v. 13). Yet when he offers to put in a good word for her with the king or the commander of the army, she refuses. Her proud words, "I live among my own people," are a testimony both to her independence and her deep distaste for charity.

Elisha must have appeared to be adding insult to injury when he then persisted with the promise: "At this season, in due time, you shall embrace a son."

One has the feeling she has been disappointed before. Why else would she immediately jump to the conclusion that this particular promise was too extravagant? Why else would she assume that the prophet was staging some cruel joke at her expense? *No, no,* we hear her thinking. *You don't understand my situation. Promise me patience, or endurance. But joy is clearly out of the question.*

Sometimes God has more in mind for us than we have in mind for ourselves. One year later the Shunammite woman did indeed embrace a son. This birth wasn't the end of her story or of her struggle toward trust, as we see if we read the sequel to this story in verses 18–37. But if the sequel shows anything, it is that she never again made the mistake of asking God for too little.

Praying for joy never occurred to me that day at the healing service. Perhaps I thought such a prayer would be too presumptuous. Or maybe, like the Shunammite woman, I didn't want to run the risk of being disappointed. But my student wasn't daunted by my depression. She just prayed. She prayed like I hadn't done in years. She prayed with reckless abandon. And before she—and God—were done with me, I was weeping. Weeping for joy, I suppose, though I could not be sure what form the joy would take. One thing is sure, however: I would never again make the mistake of asking God for too little.

I love it when my students teach me things.

For Reflection

1. Have you ever made the mistake of asking God for too little? Have you ever been "surprised by joy"?
2. What does it mean to pray, "Thy will be done"?
3. How do you handle it when God says "yes" to your prayers? when God says "no"?

Hymn Suggestions

"Lord, When I Came into This Life" (HPSS 522)
"Great God, Your Love Has Called Us Here" (HPSS 353; RIL 503; UMH 579)
"I Cannot Dance, O Love" (CH 290)

"Come, My Way, My Truth, My Life" (GC 577; H 487;
   LBW 513; NCH 331; RIL 276, 277; UMH 164)
"Lord of All Hopefulness" (GC 578; LBW 469; PsH
   558)
"I Love the Lord" (HPSS 362; NCH 511; SNC 227)
"In Thee Is Gladness" (LBW 552; PsH 566; UMH 169)

Practicing the Faith

An Undivided Heart

Psalm 86

*T*hey call them foxhole conversions, those faith commitments made when shells are exploding overhead and death looms large on the horizon. Some of these conversions undoubtedly stick. Yet, when the immediate danger is past, for some people the durability of the commitment passes as well. If God were to take us to task for our insincerity, a good lawyer could probably get us off by pleading "severe mental stress" or "temporary insanity."

Even if we did not come to Christ this way, most of us have struck the occasional bargain with God. The contract usually reads, "Please, God, if you just get me out of this mess I will. . . ." You fill in the blank.

Psalm 86 occasionally reads a little like this, especially in verse 11. "Teach me your way, O LORD, that I may walk in your truth; give me an undivided heart to revere your name." At first glance, this prayer seems like just another attempt to twist God's arm (see also Ps. 30:9). "Look God," says the psalmist. "It's really in your best interest to grant my request, since I'm going to be really, really good if you do."

Certainly the person who wrote Psalm 86 was in a tight spot. "Preserve my life," he pleads in verse 2. Later in verse 14 he says, "the insolent rise up against me; a band of ruffians seeks my life," yet a closer look at the psalm as a whole—and verse 11 in particular—sets this prayer apart from the foxhole variety.

First, the person who prayed this prayer clearly had a deeply personal relationship with God already. "I am devoted to you," he reminds God in verse 2. "You are *my* God" (italics added). And so the relationship is evidently not a new one. Verse 16 suggests that it may have begun at his mother's knee. "Save the child of your serving girl," he begs. In other words, "If you won't do it for me, do it for my mom's sake! She's served you loyally for more years than I have."

Something else sets this prayer apart. The request for an "undivided heart" in verse 11 reveals a remarkable level of realism and commitment. In fact, once we realize the cost of such a commitment, we may wonder whether we would have the courage to pray this prayer ourselves.

The "heart" in Hebrew is not only the site of the emotions, but of the intellect and the will as well. People felt, thought, and made commitments with their heart. If, heaven forbid, their heart should become "hardened," that meant they could neither think, feel, nor decide straight (which explains a lot about the Pharaoh's behavior in the Exodus story).

An undivided heart is a heart that is wholly given over to God. No corner of life is somehow kept back . . . no compartmentalization of "God's business" and "my business." Every aspect of our lives is fair game for God.

In her unconventional conversion story, *Traveling Mercies* (Pantheon Books, 1999), Anne Lamott compares Christ to a little cat running along at her heels, begging to be picked up, mewing at the door to be let in. "But I knew what would happen," she complains. "You let a cat in one time, give it a little milk, and then it stays forever" (50).

So much for the hound of heaven! Yet Lamott is on to something, not just about conversion, but about the Christian life. The mewing doesn't stop once the kitten comes through the door. Once through, we may well expect to hear mewing at some inconvenient times and in some unexpected places. And it won't stop until it's attended to.

"Into my heart, into my heart," invites the old Sunday school song. "Come into my heart, Lord Jesus. Come in today, come in to stay. Come into my heart, Lord Jesus."

Did any of us know what we were getting into when we sang that song? Probably not. Did the psalmist know what he was getting into when he prayed his prayer for an undivided heart? Who knows? But we know now. The only question is, are we really ready to make that kind of a commitment?

For Reflection

1. Did you know what you were getting into when you committed your life to Christ? What has surprised you?
2. Have you ever tried to bargain with God?
3. What would it mean for you to commit your intellect, your emotions, and your decisions to God? Are you ready to make that kind of commitment?

Hymn Suggestions

"Take My Life" (CH 609; H 707; HPSS 391; LBW 406; NCH 448; PsH 288, 289; RIL 475; UMH 399)

"Called as Partners in Christ's Service" (CH 453; HPSS 343; NCH 495)

"Santo, Santo, Santo" (CH 111; SNC 19)

"Into My Heart" (CH 304)

"I Bind My Heart" (CH 350; GC 668)

"Take, O Take Me As I Am" (SNC 215)

The Problem with Pooh

Genesis 1:24–31

*T*he only reason honey is made is for me to eat it." Thus sayeth the bear . . . Pooh Bear to be precise.

Far be it from me to pick a fight with Winnie the Pooh. I have spent many appreciative hours in the company of A. A. Milne's quirky, cuddly character. Yet, at the risk of inviting irate letters telling me to pick on somebody my own size, I can't help thinking that Pooh's attitude is problematic.

Does nature exist solely for us to consume it? No. No more than honey is made only for one hungry (albeit adorable) bear to eat it. Yet, judging from the way we have treated the world, one could easily come to that conclusion. To make matters worse, we have sometimes cited Scripture in defense of our actions. God's command to "subdue" the earth and to "have dominion" over its creatures has often been taken as a license to ransack creation for our own ends.

Clearly, if we look to the context of God's command, this reading is a tragic misinterpretation. Just before the order is issued, humanity is created in God's own image, which is hardly an insignificant detail, especially when one considers the loving majesty of the creation story so far. Each day is earmarked by some new miracle, sprung from God's fertile imagination. As the parade of creation passes by, God sits back in satisfaction, pronouncing it good, good, and *very* good. To be created in the image of this God leaves little room for random acts of selfish appetite. So "dominion" must mean something else. Walter Brueggemann is surely on the right track when he suggests that "the task of 'dominion' does not have to do with exploitation and abuse. It has to do with securing the well-being of every other creature and bringing the promise of each to full fruition" (*Genesis* [Louisville, Ky.: Westminster/John Knox Press, 1982], 32).

As if to guard against sinister distortions, the Bible's second creation story chooses its words very carefully. In Genesis 2, we read that God puts Adam in the garden and instructs him "to till it and to keep it." If any doubt remains about the nature of our relationship to nature, this statement surely dispels it. We are to "keep" the earth even as a good shepherd "keeps" his sheep. If we bear in mind the model of Jesus, the Good Shepherd, we are reminded of just how selfless this job description is. Brueggeman again writes, "It is the task of the shepherd not to control but to lay down his life for the sheep (John 10:11)."

Yet, if we are not careful, we could easily become ensnared in another misinterpretation of this ancient story. Notice, for instance, how easily we can discuss "nature" or "creation" as if we were somehow distinct from it. Nothing could be further from the truth, nor more dangerous to creation's care. We may be created in the image of God. We may even be the "crown" of creation. But we are still very much a part of creation, and our destiny is intimately connected to its own.

Perhaps another ancient story will serve to illustrate this point.

An ancient Greek story tells of Erysichthon, a man who, without a qualm, cut down every tree in the sacred grove of Ceres to feed his own insatiable greed. Ceres "pondered how to make his death a parable of her anger," and finally found the perfect way to make the punishment fit the crime. (Quotes in this story are from Ted Hughes's translation, *Tales from Ovid* [New York: Farrar, Straus, Giroux, 1997].)

She condemned Erysichthon to hunger—infinite, insatiable hunger. He devoured everything, even selling his daughter at the market "to feed the famine in her father." But none of it, of course, was enough. Finally, when nothing else could satisfy his cravings, "he began to savage his own limbs. And there, at a final feast, devoured himself."

This ugly end to an ugly story points out the peril of our aggressive and irresponsible attitudes. If we think we can continue to devour creation without finally devouring ourselves, then we deceive ourselves and the truth is not in us. When we savage creation, we savage our own limbs, and in a final feast, we threaten to devour ourselves. They don't call us "consumers" for nothing.

Perhaps the only reason nature is made is *not* for us to consume it. Perhaps it exists as well to glorify God. Maybe when the trees of the field clap their hands, God sits back and smiles, thinking, "It is good, it is good, it is *very* good." In any case, we must begin to think of our role in creation as one of responsibility rather than privilege. Pooh's attitude may be perfectly appropriate for a young bear, but it is hardly appropriate for grown-up people. Particularly grown-up Christian people.

For Reflection

1. Do you tend to think of yourself as part of nature or apart from it? How might seeing yourself as a part of God's creation influence your behavior?
2. Think about what you typically consume in a day, in a week, and in a year. What changes could you make to be a better "keeper" of creation?
3. What changes could your congregation make? Your country?

Hymn Suggestions

"Thank You, God, for Water, Soil, and Air" (HPSS 266; PsH 437; RIL 22)

"Today We All Are Called to Be Disciples" (HPSS 434)

"Touch the Earth Lightly" (CH 693; NCH 569)

"We Are Not Our Own" (CH 689)

"We Cannot Own the Sunlit Sky" (GC 710; NCH 563)

"Father Eternal, Ruler of Creation" (H 573; LBW 413; RIL 489)

"Children From Your Vast Creation" (SNC 58)

"Let There Be Light" (UMH 440)

The Courage to Be

Job 42

*I*n his famous soliloquy, Hamlet ponders whether "to be or not to be" is better. Job must surely have wondered as well. His story is one of love's labors lost. Everything he has is swept away in chapter 1. He spends the next forty chapters trying to learn one of life's hardest lessons: that righteousness is not always rewarded.

Nothing in the popular doctrines of his time could have prepared him for this. His friends rally around to remind him of the rules of reward and punishment. If you obey, you are blessed; if you sin, you suffer. Life is as simple as that, they insist. So simple, in fact, that you can even calculate the equation backwards. Where there's smoke, there's fire, after all. If you're suffering, you must have sinned. With that comforting thought, they all dance around the moonlit gazebo singing, "Somewhere in your youth or childhood, you must have done something bad."

Nothing has changed much in the ensuing centuries. Three millennia later we're still sitting in hospital waiting rooms wondering, "What did I do to deserve this?" Yet, the book of Job cautions us against such calculations. As one character in Barbara Kingsolver's novel *The Poisonwood Bible* puts it, "Don't try to make life a mathematics problem with yourself in the center and everything coming out equal" ([New York: HarperCollins, 1998], 309). Job alerts us to the fact that sometimes there is a correlation between righteousness and reward . . . and sometimes there isn't. Only God is in a position to judge the difference. Finally, we must serve God not for what we will get out of it, but simply because it is the right thing to do.

Given that the book of Job invests forty-one chapters making this point, many people think it odd that the last chapter seems to pull the rug out from under it. Job's riches are not only restored, but doubled. Wonder of wonders, even the children are replaced.

This restoration presents some logical problems. For instance, it is not possible to "replace" a lost child. And the theological problems are even more vexing. Many have maintained that the "happily ever after" ending actually undercuts the point of the book. Job's restoration seems to affirm the traditional stance of the friends, rewarding Job for good behavior. As a result, many interpreters have concluded that someone who completely missed the point tacked the epilogue onto the book. Or might there be another way to understand this enigmatic ending?

The title of this reading ("The Courage to Be") is borrowed from Paul Tillich's famous book of the same name. Tillich characterized the modern age as one consumed with anxiety. At the heart of this anxiety is the loss of a sense of life's meaning. In the face of such anxiety and loss, the very act of being requires an act of considerable courage—and, finally, faith.

If we approach the ending of the book of Job with Tillich's insights in mind, the "happy ending" may look rather different. In view of Job's experiences, we could say that Job needed far more courage "to be" than "not to be." Old Testament scholar Ellen Davis underscores this point when she calls the epilogue

a portrait of tenacious faith, stunning not so much for its reward as for its cost. For what must it have cost Job, who had been stripped to the bone and borne it . . . to "reinvest" in family and community life, with its obligations, ethical ambiguities, and terrible risks? (from "Job and Jacob: The Integrity of Faith," in *Reading In Between Texts*, ed. Danna Nolan Fewell [Louisville, Ky.: Westminster/John Knox Press, 1992], 219)

Anyone who has experienced a profound loss can testify to the kind of "tenacious faith" portrayed in the epilogue. It takes far more courage to love again when we know what losing that love means. For this reason, perhaps, Davis has referred to Job elsewhere as "the fiercest believer in the Bible."

Recognizing the fierceness of Job's faith in the rest of the book that bears his name is easy. But that fierce faith is active in the epilogue as well. Maybe his faith burns more brightly there than anywhere else—bright enough to shine like a beacon for believers across the centuries, bright enough to give us all the courage to be.

For Reflection

1. How do you feel about the ending to the book of Job?
2. Do you expect God to reward you for good behavior? punish you for bad behavior?
3. What are the risks of assuming that suffering is always a form of punishment from God? Have such assumptions ever hurt you?

Hymn Suggestions

"By Gracious Powers" (H 695, 696; HPSS 342; NCH 413; RIL 55; UMH 517) *Note that the author is Dietrich Bonhoeffer.*

"From Noon of Joy to Night of Doubt" (RIL 160)

"Let Hope and Sorrow Now Unite" (CH 639)
"You Are Mine" (GC 649)
"Your Kingdom Come" (LBW 376)
Various Settings of Psalm 130 (HPSS 240; LBW 295;
    PsH 256; RIL 134; SNC 62)

Peeking at the Last Page

Revelation 1:4–8

I once heard a seminary president make a shocking confession. With a job that entails a high level of both travel and stress, he often seeks relief from both by burying himself in the pages of a murder mystery. While there is nothing so shocking in this, to hear him tell the next part, one would think he'd committed the murder himself. After making sure there are no witnesses, he *peeks at the last page*. He doesn't need any more stress in his life, he explains guiltily. So he looks ahead just long enough to make sure that everything turns out all right. Once he's sure that his favorite characters survive, he returns to watch the plot unfold, content to wonder how—and not whether—things turn out well.

In a very real sense, the book of Revelation functions the same way for believers. In the midst of injustice and pain and loss, we read Revelation and are reassured that God's justice will triumph in the end. Everything *will* turn out all right.

Wait a minute, you may say. What is reassuring about a book so full of fire and brimstone? To hear the television prophets tell it, most of us are headed for hell, and Revelation is the road map.

Unfortunately, mainline Christian churches have largely relinquished the book of Revelation to preachers who fundamentally misunderstand the book (pun intended). If we in the mainline had the courage to reclaim John's ancient vision of Christ's return, we might discover both comfort and courage for the new millennium.

The first clue to unraveling this mystery is to stand where John stood when God first granted him this revelation. Exiled to the isle of Patmos "because of the word of God and the testimony of Jesus" (1:9), John feels the pain of the persecuted Church with peculiar clarity. From where he stands, hell is already here. The righteous suffer and the wicked prosper. Yet, we do not sense despair in what he writes. Far from it. God has given him a peek at the last page, and he writes that vision down to give us all the same reassuring glimpse.

John begins his letter with grace and peace—a tough order under the circumstances (1:4). Yet, he grounds his confidence in Jesus Christ, the "faithful witness." The Greek word for "witness" is *martus*, already well on its way to our word "martyr." John is reminding Christians tempted to renounce their faith that Jesus was the martyr who was faithful to the bitter end. For people under so much pressure to save their skin at the expense of their soul, this reminder must have been both reassuring and encouraging.

John also calls Jesus Christ "the ruler of the kings of the earth" (v. 5). This assessment also would have packed a rhetorical punch as a reminder that, all appearances to the contrary, Caesar would someday have to account for his actions to the King of Kings.

But the real reassurance comes in verse 7. "Look!" John shouts, pointing toward the heavens. "He is coming with the clouds; every eye will see him, even those who pierced him." This vision is of the triumph of God's justice, a justice so clear that even the eyes of the executioners will see it. Power will change hands. As the prophet Amos puts it, "[J]ustice [will] roll down like waters, and righteousness like an ever-flowing stream" (Amos 5:24).

Echoes of this expectation appear throughout Scripture. Isaiah 40:5 anticipates it with the words, "Then the glory of the LORD shall be revealed, and all people shall see it together." Psalm 75:2 hints, "At the set time that I appoint, I will judge with equity." And Psalm 96 celebrates the moment when God will "judge with equity" in no uncertain terms:

> Let the heavens be glad, and let the earth rejoice.
>   let the sea roar, and all that fills it;
>   let the field exult, and everything in it.
> Then shall all the trees of the forest sing for joy
>   before the LORD; for he is coming,
>   for he is coming to judge the earth.
> He will judge the world with righteousness,
>   and the peoples with his truth.
>
> (Psalm 96:11–13)

Everything about Christ's return urges reassurance rather than dread for the believer. While many of us may not feel the threat of persecution in quite the same way as the early Christians, we still feel the stress of living in a world where justice is mocked and there is often no reward for doing the right thing. "How long?" we still ask with the psalmist. "How long must I bear pain in my soul, and have sorrow in my heart all day long?" (Ps. 13:2).

Not long now, the book of Revelation reassures us. Christ is coming. Christ is coming soon (Rev. 22:20).

Having had our peek at the last page, we can sigh and say, "Amen. Come, Lord Jesus!"

For Reflection

1. A wise Christian once gave this advice about reading the book of Revelation: "Visualize, don't analyze." Do you agree with this advice? Does it help you to understand the book any better?

2. What do and don't modern Christians have in common with the early Christians whom John was addressing in the book of Revelation? What difference might that make in how we respond to it?

3. Are you looking forward to the return of Jesus Christ? Why or why not?

Hymn Suggestions

"Love Divine, All Loves Excelling" (CH 517; GC 622; H 657; HPSS 376; LBW 315; NCH 43; PsH 568; RIL 464; UMH 384)

"Joy to the World!" (CH 143; GC 343; H 100; HPSS 40; LBW 39; NCH 132; PsH 337; RIL 198; UMH 246)

"View the Present Through the Promise" (SNC 90)

Distressed Christians

Matthew 14:1–20

*T*ension crackles around the television set as we await the verdict of the expert. The program is the popular *Antiques Road Show*. The hopeful young couple fidgets nervously as the antiques dealer gets ready to announce the worth of Great-Aunt Gertie's cherished dresser. "Five hundred dollars," the dealer says dryly, "though it would be worth ten times as much if you hadn't refinished it."

I've never understood this. Why is a dingy old piece of furniture worth more than one that has been restored to its original splendor? Even more puzzling is the practice of intentionally "distressing" new furniture to make it look old. When I'm lucky enough to have something new, the last thing that occurs to me is to go at it with a hammer!

The same peculiar logic seems to be at play in this strange sequence of stories in Matthew 14. While clearly "distressed" by the murder of John the Baptist, Jesus barely has time to grieve John's grisly death. The crowds pursue him like relentless reporters, inflicting the suffering Savior with their own agenda.

Nobody could have blamed Jesus if he had told them all to go jump in the nearby lake. Yet, the Scripture says he "had compassion for them and cured their sick." Then, not content to cure them, he fed them as well. Five thousand men plus women and children dined that day on what had looked like a meager meal: five loaves and two fish. Once again, Jesus transformed the situation, turning suffering into celebration.

The sequence of these stories is likely not an accident. Matthew seems to be trying to tell us something, not just about Jesus, but about the Christian life.

Think back to the beginning of the story. Jesus had just lost John—a close friend, a cousin, and the herald of the coming Christ—yet out of Jesus' sorrow springs great compassion. Could his own sorrow have sensitized him to the suffering of those around him? As he looked out at the crowd through his own tears, did he see the tears of others? Did he understand that they had carried their friends and loved ones out into this secluded place, hoping to avoid the grief that he now knew?

Logic leads us to another, more perplexing question: Did God design Jesus' personal suffering to quicken his sense of compassion for others? For that matter, does God intentionally "distress" us to make us more valuable in the process?

If the book of Job could not solve the problem of human suffering in forty-two chapters, I'm certainly not going to try to do it in a few paragraphs. The question of why "bad things happen to good people" is far too complex for that. Yet, I will venture an observation based on the Bible and my own experience. Sometimes, by the grace of God, grief does beget compassion, and sometimes Christians who have been "distressed" by tragedy or hardship are made immeasurably valuable. The compassion they learn in the process is multiplied—like loaves and fishes—to heal and feed everyone around them.

Life doesn't always work that way, of course. Sometimes "distressed" Christians simply turn bitter and are a bane to everyone around them, including themselves. Jesus would certainly have compassion on these wounded souls as well. But he must surely smile through his tears when one of these suffering servants grows through grief and becomes even more valuable because of it.

A couple I know lost their twenty-two-year-old son to cancer a couple of decades ago. To label their experience a blessing would be absurd. Yet blessing has blossomed from it. In the years since their son's death, they have been a haven of comfort and care for other "distressed Christians." Many of us who have sought them out have been blessed by their compassion. They listen better than most people do. They aren't afraid to cry, and they aren't uncomfortable when we do. Perhaps best of all, they don't try to make the tears go away with simple answers.

Do you know anyone like this couple? Has your grief ever made you grow?

Only God knows how and why this works. But we can be very glad that—in the mercy and mystery of God—it often does.

For Reflection

1. How do you respond to suffering? Think of Christians you know who have suffered. How did they respond?
2. Has your grief ever made you grow?
3. Revisit the story about Theresa of Avilla in this book's preface. What would you say to Theresa if you had the chance?

Hymn Suggestions

"For All the Saints" (CH 637; GC 793; H 287; HPSS 526; LBW 174; PsH 505; NCH 299; RIL 397; UMH 711; cf. SNC 195)

"When a Poor One" (CH 662; HPSS 407; UMH 434)

Portrait of a Dysfunctional Family

Genesis 26:34–35; 27:46–28:5

*I*t wasn't the first time Rebekah had wondered whether life was worth living. Ever since the twins, Jacob and Esau, had staged a wrestling match in her womb, she had had her doubts (Gen. 25:22). The boys had been at each other's throats ever since. But the last straw was when Esau had up and married two Hittite women. The Bible bluntly records that these two "made life bitter" for both Isaac and Rebekah—so bitter, in fact, that Rebekah complains again that she is weary of her life.

One wonders if the Hittite holy book records another side to this story. Did Esau's wives, Judith and Basemath, have a few sharp words to say about their in-laws? Did Judith and Basemath ever wonder whether *their* lives were worth living since marrying into the Old Testament's most famous dysfunctional family?

We will never know. All we know is that *our* holy book records this family's foibles with remarkable candor. No editorial airbrush whisks away their faults, their fights, or their jealous fits of rage. For people on the lookout for role models, this characterization can be quite frustrating. Yet the biblical author seems less concerned about providing us with stained-glass saints than giving us an actual, unretouched photo of some very fallible people. In truth, this section of Genesis resembles nothing so much as a portrait of a dysfunctional family.

If their story didn't feel so familiar, we might call it tragic. But the story does feel familiar . . . too familiar. We all know the bitter taste of family discord. Whether we think of our immediate family, or the church, or—for that matter—the whole human family the faces in this portrait look startlingly familiar.

Precisely because the picture is so familiar, it may be hard to feel this biblical family's tragedy. Nineteenth-century novelist George Eliot notes that people aren't deeply moved by what is not unusual (*Middlemarch*, chap. 20). If a hurricane hits, no problem. Tears well up as we watch the news; we send charitable contributions. Maybe we even spend a couple of hours assembling health kits for the unfortunate victims. But to the familiar face of tragedy next door, we are often blind, deaf, and numb.

George Eliot again observes:

> That element of tragedy which lies in the very fact of frequency, has not yet wrought itself into the coarse emotion of [human]kind; and perhaps our frames could hardly bear much of it. If we had a keen vision and feeling of all ordinary human life, it would be like hearing the grass grow and the squirrel's heart beat, and we should die of that roar which lies on the other side of silence. As it is, the quickest of us walk about well wadded with stupidity.

Still, hear the good news: God is not so "well wadded." God *does* hear. God *does* see . . . *keenly*. The Bible is shot through with stories about it. "I have seen the misery of my people who are in Egypt," God says to a terrified shepherd on the side of Mt. Sinai. "I have heard their cry on account of their taskmasters. Indeed, I know their sufferings, and I have come down to deliver them" (Exod. 3:7–8). And that is the really remarkable part. God not only sees, hears, and knows—but God cares. God cares enough to wade into the morass of human weakness and save us from ourselves.

Who would have thought that God would bother about Isaac and Rebekah's dysfunctional family? The beauty of this Bible story, though, is that God not only bothers about it, but uses it as a springboard for blessing the whole human family. Hollywood could not have come up with a more surprising script. Rebekah's feud with her daughters-in-law serves as the excuse to send Jacob off in search of a more suitable spouse (and to escape the wrath of his freshly swindled brother, Esau). Yet, the path into exile turns out to be the road to the fulfillment of God's promise. This story is a weird but wonderful illustration of God's ability to turn bitterness into blessing.

There is something acutely comforting about this story. Yet, there is something acutely challenging about it, too. Perhaps it is calling us to move past our own imperfections and go on with the work of being a blessing. Perhaps the story is asking us to be a little more tolerant of the people whose blemishes are spoiling the family portrait. Perhaps the story is prodding us to listen a little harder for the roar of human suffering that lies just on the other side of silence.

Or perhaps this story is unable to do any of these things— because we're too "well wadded" to let it.

For Reflection

1. How sensitive are you to the suffering of others? Would you describe yourself as a) well-wadded, b) lightly padded, or c) thin-skinned? What are some of the challenges that come with each condition?
2. Compare/contrast your own family with the one described in these passages from Genesis.
3. What are the signs that God does see, hear, and care about your family? the family of the faithful? the whole human family?

Hymn Suggestions

"Where Cross the Crowded Ways of Life" (CH 665; H
    609; HPSS 408; LBW 429; PsH 602; RIL 482; UMH
    427)

"Open My Eyes That I May See" (CH 586; HPSS 324;
    UMH 454)

"Where True Love and Charity Are Found/Ubi Caritas"
    (GC 631; NCH 396)

"Open Our Eyes" (SNC 263)

"Thank Our God for Sisters, Brothers" (NCH 397)

Hostages of Hate

Luke 15:11–32

*M*om, Melissa hit me!" wailed the aggrieved voice from the family room.

The newspaper stirred slightly and the weary mother behind it sighed. Was it worth walking to the other room to referee? She hated getting caught in the middle of these things. Why couldn't they work these things out for themselves? Or better yet, not get into them in the first place? She opted to stay where she was.

"Melissa, did you hit your brother?" she called.

"Yes, but he. . . ."

"Did you hit your brother?"

"Yes," the truculent voice confessed.

"Tell him you're sorry."

Silence. The mother lowered the paper and listened until, at last, she heard the barely audible apology. "Good," she thought, going back to her reading.

But before long, the aggrieved voice piped up once more, "Mom, I don't think she meant it!"

❧❧❧❧❧❧❧

Forgiving someone is much easier if we're sure that they're sorry. But more often than not, it's hard to tell. Even if they've said the words, we can never be sure it's more than lip service.

99

The older brother in the story of the prodigal son is in a similar bind. Actually, he may have it even worse, since if we read the story carefully, he never actually hears his brother's eloquent confession: "Father, I have sinned against heaven and before you; I am no longer worthy to be called your son" (Luke 15:21).

Put yourself in the elder brother's shoes. "Junior" had convinced their father to cough up his half of the inheritance, and then disappeared to do goodness-knows-what. All that was certain was that he, the obedient older brother, had been working like a slave on his father's farm. In fact, he'd been coming in from the field when he heard the sounds of a serious party coming from the house. Who was it for? Why hadn't he been invited?

He'd had to ask one of the servants what was happening. As if that hadn't been humiliating enough, the servant had announced the "good news": Junior was back, and Dad had fired up the barbecue pit and hired a band.

Commentators have criticized the older brother for his arrogant and unforgiving attitude. Yet, we often overlook the fact that he is being asked to forgive without any certain knowledge of his brother's repentance. From his perspective, the prodigal brother seems to have just shown up, acting as if nothing is wrong. How would you feel?

Most of us would feel anger . . . perhaps even hate. What's more, since those feelings had probably been simmering for some time, the welcome home party would likely bring them to a rolling boil.

In a perfect world, every act of forgiveness would be preceded by a sincere apology. But the world does not always work that way. Victims of rape and abuse have to go on living with or without the repentance of their abusers. Sometimes death steps in and precludes the possibility of repentance, and the living victims are left with nowhere to carry their rage. Is any alternative available in such situations, other than to let the rage and resentment build to the boiling point?

Jesus showed us a more excellent, though by no means easier, way. As he was dying on the cross, he prayed this prayer for us, his executioners: "Father, forgive them; for they do not know what they are doing" (Luke 23:34). Notice that his forgiveness is not contingent upon our realizing the scope of our crime or asking for our victim's forgiveness. He simply forgives.

Colossians 3:13 counsels us to forgive "just as Christ has forgiven you." True, it isn't easy. But it is better than being held hostage by hate.

For Reflection

1. How do you handle it when you are unsure of the sincerity of someone's apology? or if someone does not apologize at all?
2. Have you ever been held hostage by hate? What did/ does it feel like?
3. What for you is the hardest thing about forgiving? about being forgiven?

Hymn Suggestions

"Forgive Our Sins as We Forgive" (GC 879; H 674; HPSS 347; LBW 307; PsH 266; UMH 390; cf. SNC 59)

"Seeking Water, Seeking Shelter" (RIL 101)

"Help Us Accept Each Other" (CH 487; HPSS 358; NCH 388; UMH 560)

What Pirates and Christians Have in Common

Colossians 3:12–17

*T*he title of this reading is the question posed by the classic *VeggieTales* song, "The Pirates Who Don't Do Anything." (If you are unfamiliar with the *VeggieTales* series, ask anyone at your church under the age of sixteen to introduce you to Larry the Cucumber and his friends.) This particular segment features a bunch of vegetables dressed up as pirates, sitting around in their recliners, singing a song about how they don't do anything remotely pirate-like anymore. They brag, for instance, that they never swab the poop deck and they never veer to starboard. In fact, they never sail at all. As they pass the potato chips, they break into their swashbuckling theme song:

> *We are the pirates who don't do anything*
> *We just stay home and lie around*
> *And if you ask us to do anything*
> *We'll just tell you, "We don't do anything!"*

While this piece pretends to be just another "silly song with Larry," it actually poses a fairly important question for Christians. Are Christians still Christians if they don't do Christian "stuff" anymore?

Colossians 3:1–17 suggests that practicing the faith means a lot more than just putting on a Christian costume. In this passage Paul urges us, along with the believers at Colossae, to clothe ourselves with compassion, kindness, humility, meekness, patience, forgiveness, peace, and above all, love. "Let the word of God dwell in you richly," he says. "And whatever you do, in word or deed, do everything in the name of the Lord Jesus, giving thanks to God the Father through him."

Notice that the wardrobe Paul recommends is more than skin deep. Qualities like kindness and humility are not the kinds of things that we slap on with our makeup in the morning. They are built up from the inside out over long periods of hard labor, much like muscles in a weight room.

While they may masquerade as nouns, all of these qualities eventually come out as verbs. Patience, for instance, is an action word. A woman I know once told me that she had learned this lesson when going through a divorce, and she had the scars to prove it. Worried, I asked her what she meant. She explained—patiently, of course—"From all the times I had to bite my tongue!"

The pirate song reminds us that merely calling ourselves Christians is not enough. Paul reminds us that doing Christian "stuff" requires a lot of hard work. If we are, indeed, to "let the word of God dwell in us richly," more will be involved than what happens on Sunday morning. The labor will involve a lifetime of disciplined Bible study and prayer, of serious social action, and the kind of internal overhaul that only the Holy Spirit can help us undertake.

Of course, if we don't like it, consider the alternative. We could become the Christians who don't do anything. For those of us who opt for simply wearing the Christian costume and not doing any of the genuine Christian "stuff," let me suggest the following theme song:

> *Refrain: We are the Christians who don't do anything*
> *We just stay home and lie around*
> *And if you ask us to do anything*
> *We'll just tell you, "We don't do anything."*

Verse: Oh, we never show compassion
And we never read the Bible
And we never pray the Lord's Prayer
Or recite the hundredth psalm
And we never feed the hungry
And we never love our neighbor
And we can't distinguish Esther from St. Paul.
(Repeat refrain once more with feeling . . .
and pass the potato chips.)

For Reflection

1. What impression would your non-Christian friends have of Christianity if your words and actions were the only thing they had to go by?
2. If we are saved by grace and not by works (Eph. 2:8–9), why do Christians have to worry about what they do and say?
3. What Christian behavior is the hardest for you to practice consistently?

Hymn Suggestions

"O Master, Let Me Walk with Thee" (CH 602; H 659, 660; HPSS 357; LBW 492; PsH 573; RIL 428; UMH 430)

"We Are Your People" (HPSS 436; NCH 309; RIL 419)

"We Call Ourselves Disciples" (CH 357)

"We Are Called" (GC 718)

"Sing! A New Creation" (SNC 241)

Misery Needs Company

Psalm 137

*J*ohn Calvin once called the Psalms a "mirror of the soul." If that's true, then Psalm 137 confronts us with a frightening reflection. "O daughter Babylon," it hisses from the heart of darkness, "Happy shall they be who pay you back what you have done to us! Happy shall they be who take your little ones and dash them against the rock!"

Our first instinct is to push this unsavory psalm away—to deny that it reflects any aspect of who we are. "It shouldn't even be in the Bible," we bluster. "Surely, someone must have slipped up when they included *this* in the canon!"

Indeed, the psalm does seem to reflect badly on people who call this book "good," whether we are Jewish or Christian. Finally, even God's image is sullied. By what stretch of the imagination, we may well ask, does this deserve to be called God's word?

I, too, was ready to turn and run from all the unpleasant images in this psalm's mirror. But then one of my students taught me how to see it with new eyes.

Rowland was giving a presentation on Psalm 137 in my seminary course on the Psalms. As he read it, he began to weep. Through the tears he told us about his years as a missionary in Malawi. He had worked there among the refugees who had flooded over the border from war-torn Mozambique. They had brought with them a litany of horror stories: young boys kidnapped and forced to kill their own families as an initiation into the army, torture as a routine method of extracting information about the hiding places of neighbors and friends. But the worst testimony of terror was from the women who had watched their own babies thrown into the large wooden mortars used for grinding corn. Threatened with the torture and death of other family members, these women were given the heavy, clublike pestles and forced to kill their own children.

With this horrific background we listened as Rowland read his paraphrase of Psalm 137:

> By the creeks of Malawi
> there we lay down and wailed when we remembered
>   Mozambique.
> In the acacia trees there we hung up our drums.
> For there our kidnappers forced us to play for them.
> Our torturers demanded a dance: "Sing us one of your
>   hymns!"
> How could we sing our hymns as refugees?
> If I forget you, O Mozambique,
> then let me forget how to play the drum.
> Let me lose my singing voice if I do not remember you,
> if I do not lift up the Church as my greatest joy.
> Hold it against Renamo and Frelimo,* O God,
> what they both said the day our hometown fell:
> "Burn it, burn it up till nothing is left."
> O descendants of terrorists, you who are doomed,
> Happy is the one that repays you an eye for an eye:
> Happy is the one that steals your babies and pounds
>   them like corn.
>   (A paraphrase of Psalm 137 by Rowland Van Es Jr.)

Suddenly, this psalm felt a lot different. Now, looking back on the experience, I realize that part of the reason for the

---

*The two opposing sides in the Mozambican civil war.

change was where we were "standing" as listeners. Rowland had invited us to stand beside people who had experienced things most of us can't even imagine. In doing so, he helped us to answer the question, "What would it take to make me say these words to God?" He helped us hear this ancient prayer as a timeless cry not so much for vengeance as for justice. Finally, he helped us see that others are beside us in this psalm's "mirror," people whose anguish shames us out of our cheap faith and self-absorbed spirituality.

Sometimes reading the Bible is a little like looking for real estate; the three most important things to remember are "location, location, location." When we read Psalm 137, our location is critical. If we stand apart from the exiles who spoke it all those years ago on the riverbanks of Babylon, the psalm will probably horrify us. But if we stand beside the exiles, we may hear it as an invitation to intercession and social justice. Because the truth of the matter is that the faces in the mirror beside us are not ancient, but modern. And misery, in any age, needs company.

For Reflection

1. What is the difference between a prayer for justice and a prayer for revenge? Which do you hear in this psalm? What is the author of the psalm actually praying for?
2. Are you glad this psalm is in the Bible? Why or why not?
3. What happens when we stand beside others in prayer?

Hymn Suggestions

"O for a World" (HPSS 386; NCH 575)
"O Day of God, Draw Nigh" (CH 700; H 600, 601; HPSS 452; NCH 611; RIL 178; UMH 730)

"Let Justice Roll Like a River" (GC 716; cf. NCH 588)
"Blest Be the Tie That Binds" (CH 433; HPSS 438;
   LBW 370; PsH 315; RIL 407, 408; UMH 557)
"O God Your Justice Towers" (SNC 272)

We're Being Followed

Psalm 23:6

*F*or years the annual piano recital took the bloom off my birthday. Inevitably the ordeal was scheduled for those waning weeks of May, and eager anticipation was thus checked by unadulterated dread. Visions of cakes, balloons, and presents were upstaged by nightmares of sweaty palms, awkward memory lapses, and nauseating nervousness.

My mother always claimed to enjoy these occasions. She would sit toward the back and try to match the parents to the pianists, based on blushes, coughs, and general body language. I'm glad she had a good time. I, on the other hand, would approach the bench with a martyred air, living only for the moment when the last notes were played.

I suppose my longing for those last notes made me rush. Like a horse catching sight of the barn, I would break into a musical gallop as the piece drew to a close. Whether I was playing a dirge or a scherzo, the tempo toward the end was always "lickety-split."

I have observed something of the same phenomenon in the way we read Psalm 23. Though perhaps not motivated by an anxious urge to get it over with, we have a tendency to read right over the last verse and head for the proverbial barn. Just this once, I'd like to force us to slow down and savor these familiar words: "Surely goodness and mercy shall follow me all the days of my life: and I shall dwell in the house of the LORD forever" (KJV).

I was reading a Nora Roberts novel the other day and laughed out loud when I saw the names she'd given to the heroine's golden retrievers: Goodness and Mercy. Get it? *Goodness and Mercy shall follow me. . . ?* The best part was that—unlike me—Roberts resisted the temptation to nudge her readers in the ribs by pointing out the allusion to Psalm 23. She simply slipped it in, confident that those readers who knew the psalm would get the joke.

Yet Roberts may have said more than she knew. There is something profoundly appropriate about picturing Goodness and Mercy this way. Here's why.

So often we think about the Christian life in terms of following Jesus. We strain to listen for the Good Shepherd's voice in every situation, in every decision. We follow him even through the valley of death, secure in the knowledge that he has walked that lonesome valley before and will lead us safely through.

Yet, there are times in this life after grace when we lose the will to follow God's lead. We doubt God's mercy, and we're unsure of God's direction. We wonder whether God has abandoned or betrayed us. We worry that *we* may have abandoned or betrayed God.

In these times it's good to know that the Good Shepherd has some trusty sheepdogs . . . and their names are Goodness and Mercy. Even when we stray from the path, we are being followed. In fact, the Hebrew word for "follow" can also be translated "pursue." Try that translation on for size the next time you are feeling lost or forgotten. "Surely, Goodness and Mercy shall *pursue* you all the days of your life. . . ."

This verse reminds us that our security in the faith does not depend on our own sense of clarity or confidence. Our security depends, rather, on a God whose steadfast love will not let us go.

If any hurrying is to be done in this last verse of the Twenty-third Psalm, the rush is not to the barn, but to God's house. Goodness and Mercy have been driving us there all along. It is both a destination and a dwelling place. We can hear this already/not yet quality in the various ways this last phrase is translated: "my whole life long" (NRSV) puts the emphasis on the present; "for ever" (KJV) tips our attention toward the future. In either case we will be busy. God's house, remember, is a place of worship.

Isaac Watts captures the essence of this verse in his paraphrase, "My Shepherd Will Supply My Need." "The sure provisions of my God attend me all my days," he writes. "Oh may your house be my abode, and all my work be praise." Then, taking loving liberty with the text, he adds, "There would I find a settled rest, while others go and come; no more a stranger or a guest, but like a child at home." These words are those of a man who has read slowly, a man who has felt Goodness and Mercy nipping at his heels, a man who knows we're being followed.

Thanks be to God, we're being followed.

For Reflection

1. Have you ever tried to "shake" the goodness and mercy of God? Have you ever felt like you didn't want God nosing around in your business, and wished that God would just leave you alone?
2. Christians believe that in baptism we are "marked as Christ's own forever." To what degree is it possible for baptized Christians to wander from the grace of God?
3. What is the most comforting thing about this verse for you? The most challenging?

Hymn Suggestions

"My Shepherd Will Supply My Need" (CH 80; H 664; HPSS 172; NCH 247; cf. GC 32; LBW 451; PsH 23; SNC 181)

"O Love That Wilt Not Let Me Go" (CH 540; HPSS
384; LBW 324; NCH 485; UMH 480)
"From Noon of Joy to Night of Doubt" (RIL 160)

Index of Primary
Scripture Passages